T0209292

DEEP CALLING TO DEEP

OVERCOMING THE STRUGGLES TO TRUST GOD

WILLIAM PAUL LERO

WESTBOW
P R E S S®
A DIVISION OF THOMAS NELSON
& ZONDERVAN

WestBow Press books may be ordered through booksellers or by contacting:

WestBow Press
A Division of Thomas Nelson & Zondervan
1663 Liberty Drive
Bloomington, IN 47403
www.westbowpress.com
844-714-3454

Because of the dynamic nature of the Internet, any web addresses or links contained in
this book may have changed since publication and may no longer be valid. The views
expressed in this work are solely those of the author and do not necessarily reflect the views
of the publisher, and the publisher hereby disclaims any responsibility for them.

Any people depicted in stock imagery provided by Getty Images are models,
and such images are being used for illustrative purposes only.
Certain stock imagery © Getty Images.

Scripture quotations marked (NLT) are taken from the Holy Bible, New Living Translation,
copyright ©1996, 2004, 2015 by Tyndale House Foundation. Used by permission of
Tyndale House Publishers, Carol Stream, Illinois 60188. All rights reserved.

Scripture quotations marked (NASB1995) taken from the (NASB®) New
American Standard Bible®, Copyright © 1960, 1971, 1977, 1995 by The Lockman
Foundation. Used by permission. All rights reserved. www.lockman.org

Scripture quotations marked TPT are from The Passion Translation®. Copyright © 2017, 2018, 2020
by Passion & Fire Ministries, Inc. Used by permission. All rights reserved. ThePassionTranslation.com.

Scripture quotations marked (NASB) taken from the (NASB®) New American
Standard Bible®, Copyright © 1960, 1971, 1977, 1995, 2020 by The Lockman
Foundation. Used by permission. All rights reserved. www.lockman.org

Scripture quotations marked (NIV) are taken from the Holy Bible, New International Version®,
NIV®. Copyright © 1973, 1978, 1984, 2011 by Biblica, Inc.® Used by permission of Zondervan.
All rights reserved worldwide. www.zondervan.com The "NIV" and "New International Version"
are trademarks registered in the United States Patent and Trademark Office by Biblica, Inc.®

Scripture marked (NKJV) taken from the New King James Version®. Copyright
© 1982 by Thomas Nelson. Used by permission. All rights reserved.

ISBN: 978-1-6642-8915-4 (sc)
ISBN: 978-1-6642-8916-1 (hc)
ISBN: 978-1-6642-8914-7 (e)

Library of Congress Control Number: 2023900587

Print information available on the last page.

WestBow Press rev. date: 3/15/2023

To my beautiful bride, Jeanie, you are a sweet fragrance of what the love of Jesus is really like. I could never thank you enough for your patience, prayer, and love. You are the love of my life.

To Josiah and Mike, our two rock stars. I am so proud of who you are and who you are becoming as you step into your destiny in God. You have been a true inspiration to me over the years. I love you both through and through.

To all millennials and gen Zers, especially those at Impact Church, it has been my great joy to be a part of your journey as you walk into your identity in Christ and what he has planned for you. May the truth that nothing can ever separate you from the love of God that is revealed in Christ Jesus always burn fiercely in the depths of your souls.

And finally, to Dad and Mom—though you are no longer on this earth, I honor you for your love and for the great sacrifices you made to give me a better life. I could never thank you enough.

Please Note:

The reader is strongly encouraged to read the introduction.

A general overview of books two and three of the Deeper Trilogy may be found following the afterward. All profits from the sale of book one will be donated to the work of the kingdom of God as a "first fruits" offering to the Lord.

Within chapters and at the end of each chapter you will see the Hebrew word *Selah*. Many scholars believe *Selah* was a musical term meaning "pause" or "rest" since it occurs so many times in the Psalms and the Psalms were sung. So, think of *Selah* as an invitation to pause, to take time to reflect on what has been said, how it has impacted you, and what the Spirit is saying to help you move forward in your relationship with God. Questions often follow a *Selah* to prompt you to consider digging deeper.

I have also included a suggested prayer at the end of each chapter. These prayers are simply thoughts to consider as you ponder your own personal spiritual journey. Hopefully, they will help you formulate your own prayers to God. For those who are not used to praying to God, these proposed prayers could act as a "jump-start" to get you going.

The last page of each chapter contains a summary of key points from the chapter to refresh your memory. Several more questions are also included for personal meditation or group discussions. Although you can certainly process *Deep Calling to Deep* on your own with the Holy Spirit, linking arms with friends or others in a small group will enrich this part of your journey in a big way. "Better together" is real. As you travel the trails in this book, please also consider journaling your thoughts to help you process your hurdles to trusting God.

Finally, the names and circumstances of people mentioned in the book have been significantly altered to protect their identities. Any similarities of these characters to you personally are purely coincidental.

Contents

Contents

Introduction

Trust in the Lord and do good. Then you will live safely in the land and prosper. Take delight in the Lord, and he will give you your heart's desires. Commit everything you do to the Lord. Trust him, and he will help you ... (Psalm 37:3–5, NLT)

I pray that from his glorious, unlimited resources he will give you mighty inner strength through his Holy Spirit. And I pray that Christ will be more and more at home in your hearts as you trust in Him. May your roots go down deep into the soil of God's marvelous love. And may you have the power to understand, as all God's people should, how wide, how long, how high and how deep his love really is ... Then you will be filled with the fullness of life and power that comes from God. (Ephesians 3:16–19, NLT)

Last week, I began to lose sight of the way things were supposed to be in my life. Literally. I was going blind due to a retinal tear in my left eye. Like a solar eclipse, where the moon carves a black sliver out of the sun's rays, a crescent-shaped darkness was slowly migrating across my field of vision. It was an eerie feeling, to say the least. I thank God that the retinal specialists were able to intervene in time to stop the deterioration. In fact, by the grace of God, I have recovered my sight! As I prepared for the emergency procedure, I had this peculiar mix of fear of the unknown, but also an assurance—a peace that God was with me, that it was going to turn out all right, no matter what.

Though God was not the one who caused those retinal layers to pull away from the back of my eye, he spoke to me about the whole ordeal several days later. The Lord was disciplining me, and it was intense. "Bill," he said, "you have a blind spot. I am using this to rouse you to do what I have called you to do."

I immediately knew what he was referring to. He had given me a task to complete. Though I had been working on it diligently for almost two years, I had slacked off recently to attend to other, less important matters—the ordinary things of life that keep us busy, day in and day out.

The voice continued. "No more detours. No more getting sidetracked ... You have gotten in the way of the vision I have for you. You have been a block to entering your own destiny."

Whoa! That was not an easy word to hear, but there was no condemnation in his rebuke. God was just trying to get through to me, pure and simple. My responsibility was to respond appropriately. As I meditated on all these happenings, a much-larger picture of the challenges we all face in our relationships with God began to emerge. The reality is that almost all of us have blind spots in our connections with God. It took me much too long to recognize mine. Some I had suppressed, and others—well, I just wasn't in touch with them. These are the places in the heart that we're too embarrassed to admit, too ashamed to enter into, or too afraid to explore—either with God, with others, or perhaps even with ourselves.

So, what do we do? We hide. It's kind of a variation of impostor syndrome. We try to make things look good on the outside. We don various masks, depending on whom we are with. It might be the mask of competence at work, of confidence with friends, or of joy at church. But when we withdraw into quiet solitude for a few moments to gather our "true" selves, the elusive questions of life simmer to the surface from the depths of our souls. About the lives we are living. About God. About who we are. About who we are not. About where we're headed. And if we'll ever get there.

If you're being honest with yourself, the truth is that, like me, you probably have also created "detours" or have otherwise gotten sidetracked in your relationship with God. You would like it to be better, but you know that, way down, something is off. You may not be sure exactly what it is, but it's just not right. The connection isn't as strong as you would like it to be.

As I was praying about all this, the story of the Old Testament prophet Elijah came to my mind (1 Kings 19). That passage definitely has some good "deep" for us.

After Elijah scores a stunning victory over hundreds of pagan prophets under the control of Queen Jezebel, the wicked monarch vows to take the seer's life in revenge. Thoroughly intimidated, the man of God bolts. Alone and exhausted after a two-hundred-mile trek through the desert, Elijah eventually hides in a cave on Mt. Sinai, the same mountain where Moses had encountered God centuries before. There, God speaks to him.

"Elijah, what are you doing here?" God asks.

After a response filled with self-pity and self-defense, God summons the prophet to come to the mouth of the cave. As Elijah lingers there, a tornado roars past, hurling rocks all about him. But God is not in the tornado. Then the earth heaves in random, convulsive waves, jolting the mountain in its fury. But God is not in the earthquake. Then fire streaks down from the firmament, blazing a path of destruction around the old man. But God is not in the fire. Finally, a stillness descends. From the midst of a gentle breeze, a serene whisper from the heart of God beckons the man of God a second time.

"Elijah, what are you doing … *here*? Here is not *where* you're supposed to be. Here is not *who* you're supposed to be. I have more for you, so much more. But you cannot accomplish what I have for you out here in the wilderness, hiding in the shadows of a cave. Now, go! Be the mighty man of God I have called you to be! Do what I have called you to do!"

The powerful prophet had gotten so distracted and unfocused in his relationship with God that he had forgotten who he was and who was with him.

That is how it is for many believers. Rather than leaning into God for strength to fight the various "Jezebels" who seek to subdue us in the battles of life, we retreat into caves. They are not physical caves as they were for Elijah, but caves of our own making ... *in the heart.* We believe these caverns cloak us, protect us from harm—from the tornadoes, the earthquakes, and the burning, pressing needs of life. And we hide there. Hopefully, only for a season. But tragically, for some, for a lifetime.

But here's the problem when we hide—we remain in the dark. And, worse than that, demonic elements, whose sole aim is to imprison us there, also dwell in the caves. Why? Because, if the "dragons," as I call them, can hold us captive in the caves, we will never truly learn to trust God fully, love him freely, or pursue his purposes faithfully. These demons hinder us from entering the abundance of life God desires for us. They are obstacles in our relationship with our heavenly Father.

Now, the caves in our hearts can come in all forms and sizes. On the surface, some of them may even appear noble—like spending extra time with the kids, teaching Sunday school, or working on a college degree to try to get that promotion at work. But sometimes those virtuous efforts are a distraction to keep us busy, not really drawing us any closer to our Father-God. Or the caves in the heart can be much more insidious. Caves where depression, anxiety, or confusion reign, or where addictions are expressed—alcoholism, substance abuse, porn, whatever.

But let me shake you up a bit. *Those life challenges are not the real caves.* Despite how totally overwhelming any of those mental health issues can be, they are actually side trails away from the larger caverns buried even further in "the true deep" of the heart—deeper caverns where unresolved guilt, shame, fear, offense at God, and doubt reside. Deeper caverns where we are seduced by the temptations of the world and our own flesh. That's where the bigger demons live who give rise to the depression, anxiety, and addictions we deal with. They draw us away from God like the sirens hypnotizing Ulysses away from his appointed destiny in *The Odyssey.*

xiv

Incredibly, sometimes we willingly choose to remain in the caves. Why? Because for most people, it's just a whole lot easier to stay there than to enter the painful process of exploring where our shame, fears, and offenses at God come from or why worldly temptations continue to master us. Engaging those Goliaths is long, labor-intensive work that often delivers many thorny revelations—about ourselves, our loved ones, our friends, and even the lies we have believed about God. Relatively few choose to travel that road, and fewer still complete the process. But the Spirit of God is always pursuing us, exhorting us forward with familiar, though haunting, words: "Is this all there is? Is my life passing me by and I'm missing what God has for me? Why do I have such trouble trusting him 100? What is it? What's wrong?"

We look up to the sky as if pleading with God to speak a crystal-clear, thundering word of direction to us. But God does not spin a ravaging wind about us or jar the earth beneath our feet, or send a scorching torrent from heaven to arrest our attention as he did for Elijah. He speaks to us in the intimacy of a whisper, with the exact same words he uttered to Elijah so, so long ago—words filled with great compassion, acceptance, and affirmation, enticing us into his love.

"What are you doing … *here* … in this place and in this time in your life? Here is not *where* you're supposed to be. Here is not *who* you're supposed to be. I have so much more for your life, but as long as you remain here in these caves, you will miss the fullness of my heart's desire for you."

Deep Calling to Deep: Overcoming the Struggles to Trust God, then, is meant to be a whisper from the "deep" of the kindness of God's great love to the deep need of your soul to come back to him, your one true love, and to seek him with all that is within you. No more detours. No more getting side-tracked.

Its primary aim is to unwrap the struggles we have in trusting God. If we are ever going to arrive at the place of complete trust, we need to face the dragons within our hearts head-on slay them. Victory in the battles against false guilt, shame, fear, offense, and doubt will open the door to a deeper, more vibrant, and more intimate relationship with Father-God. Success in those conflicts frees us to lay hold of our true identities in him and to grasp the purposes he planned for us even before the world began (Ephesians 2:10).

But truth be told, many of us need help getting to that place of trust. Too many things have happened. We're not always sure of who God is. And we don't always know where to start or how to undo the things that have gotten in the way. That's what *Deep Calling to Deep* is about. It will equip you to fight the dragons as you allow the light of the Holy Spirit to bring you revelation. It will guide you through the caverns and suggest questions to ask yourself as you pursue your own inner healing and the richer relationship with God that you so crave.

If you are going to grow through *Deep Calling to Deep*, you will need to set aside time to study, digest, and truly process the issues I will raise. It's not one of those fluff books you can pick up while you're in the waiting room of a dentist's office, listening to some lame background music. *Deep Calling to Deep* is for those who yearn for *transformation* more than just inspiration. Reading it will take work, prayer, some very intentional soul-seeking and, most of all, *courage*. True grit. Looking at ourselves never comes easy.

The trails through the caves? Unfortunately, over the four decades it's been since I committed my life to Christ, I have come to know them all too well. That's why I can take you there. As you listen to the gracious voice of the Holy Spirit, that's how I hope to lead you out. That's the thing with being transformed into the image of Christ—it's never over. The adventure never ends. As we surrender our hearts to God in the process, he meets us because he is fully committed to completing the good work that he has begun in us (Philippians 1:6).

One last word of encouragement—keep pushing through *Deep Calling to Deep*, however difficult and slow it may be for you to confront the dragons. There may be days that you are only able to handle a few pages. That's totally fine. There's no rush. *Just keep moving forward* at your own pace to unpack the issues. Your perseverance will bring the inner healing you seek.

So …

If you're the kind of person who is too ashamed to share the struggles of your "deep" with a friend or a counselor, but you still long to "work on your stuff" …

If you want to understand the cross and God's great grace towards you better …

If you want to shed your shame, triumph over fear, release your offense at God, or overcome doubt …

If you want to have a greater awareness of how Satan lures you into the quicksand of worldly temptations …

If you want to restore "deep" and trust in your relationship with God that maybe you haven't experienced in a long time or maybe have never experienced …

… then, *Deep Calling to Deep* is for you!

Here's the good news—you don't have to do it alone! Remember, there is a light at the mouth of the cavern. His name is Jesus, and he has promised us that when we ask, it shall be given to us. When we knock, the door shall be opened. When we seek, we *will* find the right path. Psalm 119:105 tells us that His Word is "a lamp to our feet and a light to our path" (NASB1995). Our God is faithful. He will guide us to the right trails out of the caves to experience the healing we so desire.

We have nothing to lose and everything to gain. The time has come to move forward in this life we live. Let the journey begin!

So then, my soul, why would you be depressed? Why would you sink into despair? Just keep hoping and waiting on God, your Savior. No matter what, I will still sing with praise, for you are my saving grace … *My deep need calls out to the deep kindness of your love.* Your waterfall of weeping sent waves of sorrow over my soul, carrying me away, cascading over me like a thundering cataract. All through the day Yahweh has commanded his endless love to pour over me. Through the night I sing his songs and my praises to the living God. (Psalm 42:5, 7–8, TPT; emphasis mine)

"A bruised reed He will not break and a dimly burning wick He will not extinguish …" (Isaiah 42:3, NASB1995)

Behold, You desire truth in the innermost being … (Psalm 51:6, NASB1995)

CHAPTER 1

Slaying the Demons Within: False Guilt and Shame

Do not fear, for your shame is no more. Do not be embarrassed, for you will not be disgraced. You will forget the inadequacy you felt in your youth … (Isaiah 54:4, TPT)

Behold, I lay in Zion a choice stone, a precious cornerstone, and the one who believes in Him will not be put to shame. (1 Peter 2:6, NASB)

> "I was lost and could not see
> But You did not give up on me
> To save me from my guilt and shame
> You stepped into the world You made
> And on the cross of Calvary
> You gave Your life to set me free
> Forever I will sing Your Name
> Hands high heart full of praise"

(Phil Wickham, from "Heart Full of Praise" on the album *Hymn of Heaven*, lyrics © 2021 Essential Music Publishing)

"And I know that vulnerability is the core of shame and fear and our struggle for worthiness, but it appears that it's also the birthplace of joy, of creativity, of belonging, of love." (Dr. Brené Brown)

What the Enemy Is After ...

We are about to enter the first cave. Remove your sword from its scabbard. You will need it. A dragon called false guilt and shame awaits us there, and you are going to take him out with the truth of the Word of God. *That* is your sword![1] He is the first of the demons within that you will encounter in your travels. No, I am not saying you are demon-possessed. These demons are within us only in the sense that we can hide them so easily from others, so people don't really know what's going on in our hearts. Sometimes, we can even hide them from ... ourselves. But they are there! They are at once seductive and destructive. And they will remain so, if we let them. That's why we must be diligent to seek them out.

What are the other demons we shall contend with further down the trail? Fear, offense at God, unforgiveness, and doubt, among others. Though all these creatures inhabit different caves, they are all related. They all have the same father—Satan, the father of lies himself.[2] In fact, deception is the adversary's only weapon. Every demon-dragon he dispatches is armed with a lie—lies they breathe into your mind directly. Lies they declare over you through others. And lies about God that are so persuasive, you wonder, *could that really be true?*

But take note! Here is the problem with believing lies: They tie you down. They cage you in. They suffocate who you were created to be. And that's precisely what the enemy wants to do to you. The sole purpose of his existence is to steal, kill, and destroy you—and me![3] That's it! Everything he does falls under one of those headings.

What, exactly, is this tyrant of the soul trying to steal, kill, and destroy? The tormentor goes after four things primarily:

- Relationship: Satan tries to separate you from God by distorting your image of God—who you believe God is or what you believe he has done to you. God designed life with connection foremost in mind—connection with him first, then with others. Satan, on the other hand, is the master disconnector because he himself is totally disconnected from God's love. He will do anything to keep you diverted from seeking relationship with your Creator.

- Identity: The enemy endeavors to keep you from realizing who you are in Christ, your true identity. He does this by trying to steal or choke out the covenant promises of God's Word to you.[4] Feeding the soul with the truth of the Word (the Bible) is what transforms you to become more like Jesus.[5] It is the Word that imparts life. It is the Word that empowers you to act with the authority of Jesus on this earth. Heaven and earth will pass away, but the Word of our God will never pass away.[6]

  The devil is terrified that you will discover you are royalty, a priest, a son or daughter of God Most High, and that you have the power of the Holy Spirit dwelling within you to overcome him. Then, you will live life to the fullest in God's will. Grasping the fullness of who you are in Christ will seriously hinder the adversary's destructive purposes in your life and on the earth.

- Vision and purpose: Satan tries to sidetrack you from what God has called you to do. He wants to sabotage your future and rob you of the gifts God has placed within you to bring him glory. One of the enemy's main ploys here is to tempt you with what 1 John 2:16 calls "the lust of the flesh and the lust of the eyes and the boastful pride of life" (NASB1995). Interpretation: the yearning for physical pleasure, a longing for those things you see, and pride in your achievements, possessions, or status. He entices you with vain idols so you don't tap into your one true source—God.

• Faith, hope, and love: These three ingredients are found in the last verse of "the love chapter," 1 Corinthians 13. This verse states that, when all is said and done, the three things that hold true meaning in life and that will endure to the end of time are faith, hope, and love. They are the fuel for the furnace of each of the three items listed above.

So, the destroyer tries to sow seeds of doubt into faith, to steal hope, and to cultivate fear in you. Those are his ways of killing you softly and guiding you into despair. He truly is the Antichrist! All of these have a profound impact on how we do life.

But we cannot forget the rest of the picture. Although Satan is out to kill, steal, and destroy, Jesus came to crush the works of the evil one so we might have *life!*[7] And he has already won the war through the cross and his resurrection! That is the Jesus who accompanies us now in our quest to restore what the devil has taken from us.

Come! Let us not tarry. *Now* is the time to venture forth!

Trying to Get a Grip on Guilt and Shame

Just a "Little" Shame?

We've all felt it—shame. It can be hard to put a finger on what it is sometimes, though. I remember when I was in seventh grade, my family temporarily moved to a new town just for a year so my mom could finish her university degree. If you've ever moved before, you know that you suddenly become a nobody in the new place. So, what do you do? You try to establish yourself in some way. One of the things I did was to try out for our middle school baseball team, and I made it!

I was stoked! Having been a Little League All-Star second baseman the previous two seasons, this was going to be fun—or so I thought. Skill-wise, I was maybe in the middle of the pack, but I was a *seventh* grader. Coach favored the eighth graders because there would always be "next year" for kids like me. Except there wasn't going to be a next year for me because the plan was always for our family to move back to our old hometown after Mom was done.

So, I was on the team, but I've got to be honest—I didn't really feel like I was part of the team because Coach never put me in. I sat on the bench. Every game. Every inning. The entire season. Oops! No, wait! Coach did put me in for the last inning of the last game—*in right field*. You know how many times I had ever played anywhere in the outfield in my entire life? None. Ever. I was terrified! Seriously, I remember praying as I looked *way in* at the batters through a new pair of glasses, "God, please make it

6

so nobody hits it out here to me. Please! Please! Please!" And you know, he worked it out!

Yup. One-half of an inning in the outfield. Three outs, and my season was over. I never even got to bat. All I can remember is that I felt pretty awful when I jogged back to the bench from the outfield. I didn't want to talk to anybody. I didn't even want to be there. I looked down at the ground with my glove folded in my lap. Shame. I didn't know what it was at the time, but for sure it was shame.

Okay, so that was middle school in a galaxy far, far away in a time long, long ago. You get older. You let it go. You move on. It was sort of an important deal to me as a boy back then, but in the grand scheme of life, it wasn't going to be a game changer. Or maybe it was, in a way. I never did try out for another baseball team again. Hmm.

That's our tendency when it comes to shame: we sweep it under the rug. "It's nothing," we try to convince ourselves. Over time, though, when you feel shame one time after another after another, it starts to pile up. When you sweep enough dirt under the rug, a lump forms. If that lump gets big enough, it might just trip you up later in life in ways that you aren't even aware of. Listen—it only hit me *just a few minutes ago* as I was writing this that I *never* tried out for another baseball team. See what I mean?

But keeping a bench warm that season was nothing compared to the weight Kristen carried.

Heavy Shame: Kristen's Story

Kristen was a middle-aged, casual friend I knew from playing on a co-ed volleyball team together. Unfortunately, she was now suffering from a brain tumor. She went through the usual medical protocol for her type of cancer—neurosurgery to remove as much of the tumor as possible followed by radiation. But her doctors were not optimistic about her prognosis. Even though they had given her only a few months to live, Kristen amazed everyone when she was still alive two years later. A lot of the credit for that had to go to the loving and invested support network of family and friends who regularly visited to talk, have a few laughs, and just hang out with her.

Kristen didn't live that close to us, but one sunny California afternoon I was going to be passing through her neighborhood, and I jumped at the opportunity to see her. I wasn't sure if she was a believer or not, and her neurologic condition was deteriorating more quickly now. By the grace of God, no other friends were visiting on that particular day, so I was able to have a special time with her while her husband was busy in the kitchen.

I gently probed Kristen about her belief in God and about death, knowing that this could well be my last visit with her. With slow and slightly slurred speech, she shared that she did believe in Jesus, but she felt that God had punished her with that brain tumor.

"Punished you? For what?" I was perplexed.

"Because," she hesitated, "because of what I did." There was another pause. "Before I got married … I had an abortion."

The remorse in her voice was intense, and a tear welled up in the corner of her eye. My heart sank to realize that Kristen had carried this unbearable weight for decades. I waited a few moments for both of us to recover.

"Kris," I began, "you recognize now that what you did was wrong. When we confess to God that we've messed up, he's right there, ready to forgive us. It wasn't God who gave you that tumor, and it had nothing to do with the abortion. That tumor came from the one who wants to destroy you, the devil himself, not God. And you can unload that guilt and shame you've been carrying around all these years onto Jesus. That's what the cross is all about. He wipes the slate clean for us when we bring it to him. He loves you through and through."

And that's what we did. I guided her in a prayer of confession to God, of forgiving herself, and of restoring her connection to God through Christ. The peace that came over her before I left was sweetness.

As it turned out, Kris did pass away two months later. I never did get the chance to see her alive again. But I know without a doubt that she left this world with a great expectation of walking into the loving embrace of Jesus.

So, exactly what was Kris grappling with for so long aside from the brain tumor itself? Was it guilt, shame, or both? You may also have heard of something called "false guilt." What is that all about? Many people are confused about these terms, mostly because there can be a lot of overlap between them—kind of like the Venn diagrams we learned about in geometry. But we must make some critical distinctions between them before we begin our internal house-cleaning.

All of this is so important because, now that I've gotten a little older, I can sincerely say that I have watched family members and friends carry their guilt and shame all the way to the grave. It can be so detrimental and limiting in our lives, and it is one of Satan's oldest tricks. He actually pulled out the shame bazooka right there in the garden of Eden immediately after the Fall. Look at Adam and Eve's initial response after they ate of the forbidden fruit: "At that moment their eyes were opened, and they suddenly felt shame at their nakedness. So they sewed fig leaves together to cover themselves. When the cool evening breezes were blowing, the man and his wife heard the Lord God walking about in the garden. So they hid from the Lord God among the trees" (Genesis 3: 7–8, NLT).

Isn't that fascinating? The very first recorded response of Adam and Eve to their sin was not what we might expect—fear. No, it was *shame*! The two "felt shame." Then they covered themselves to try to hide from God. That's what shame does to us: we pull back. We cover ourselves in some way. We try to hide from God, but he's so awesome that he still comes looking for us. He is so in love with us that he hates it when we feel there's something between us and him because, through Jesus, the door to him is still always open.

So, let's parse out these three: true guilt, false guilt, and shame so we know what we're talking about.

Selah. (Take time to pause.)

Reflections:

Satan is the one who comes to steal, kill, and destroy. Thinking back to the comments in this section on what the enemy is after, which area has been the most difficult for you in your journey as a follower of Christ and why?

- Your relationship to Father-God?
- Your identity in Christ?
- Figuring out the vision/purpose that God has for your life?
- Faith, hope, and love?
- All the above?
- Or you're not quite sure where things are at for you right now?

True Guilt

I have no idea why I did it, even today. It was so out of character for me and just plain dumb. At the tender age of six, I was turning into the Necco wafer bandit in my hometown!

There was a small grocery store just down the street that my mom would go to if we only needed a few things. Sometimes she would take me with her. One day, while she was at the cashier's counter, I hung back a little where the candy rack was tucked away, just out of sight. With a quick glance around to make sure no one was looking, I slipped a pack of Necco wafers into my pocket. The worst part was that I got away with it, which only encouraged me to try it again and again. Over time, I expanded the variety of my booty to several gum flavor lines—Juicy Fruit, peppermint, and wintergreen. This all continued for maybe fifteen months before I decided I really needed to knock it off.

Even at such a young age, the guilt of my sin began to hound me—for years! Really, I used to check whether or not my photo was on the FBI's "ten most-wanted" list on the post-office wall, which they used to do back then! Finally, one day about fifteen years later, when I was at college no less, I couldn't take it any longer. I put three dollars cash[8] in an envelope to cover the cost of the candy "plus interest," wrote a letter of apology to the store manager, and popped it into snail mail.

There was no way I was going to tell my roommates what I was doing and, of course, I certainly wasn't going to sign my name to any note or include a return address. But I was utterly convinced that this act of contrition was going to get me over the fear of the whole town knowing that the FBI was on an all-out manhunt to track me down. As strange as it sounds, the freedom from that burden was wonderful, even though it literally cost me only a few dollars.

That was true guilt, a good thing. Guilt is the conviction of the Holy Spirit that pricks our conscience to know when we've done something wrong, to take responsibility for our wrongdoing, and to try to rectify the situation, if that's possible. It causes us to lose our sense of peace. We feel ill at ease inside. Maybe a little anxious. We might even develop psychosomatic symptoms: a headache, a queasy stomach, perhaps a tightness in the chest. We can tell something is off; we are just not ourselves. Sometimes the guilt can be overwhelming. Listen to the words of King David after he was confronted about his affair with Bathsheba:

> Oh, what joy for those whose disobedience is forgiven, whose sin is put out of sight! Yes, what joy for those whose record the Lord has cleared of guilt, whose lives are lived in complete honesty! When I refused to confess my sin, my body wasted away, and I groaned all day long. Day and night your hand of discipline was heavy on me. My strength evaporated like water in the summer heat. Finally, I confessed all my sins to you and stopped trying to hide my guilt. I said to myself, "I will confess my rebellion to the Lord." And you forgave me! All my guilt is gone. (Psalms 32:1–5, NLT)

True guilt, then, is a red flag that we have chosen to follow our own way rather than God's way in some area of our lives. That is what sin is all about. It's a healthy kind of guilt that prompts us to acknowledge our failures and to address them.

How do we do that? David answers that question in Psalm 32 above, and 1 John 1:9 (TPT) confirms it: "But if we freely admit our sins when his light uncovers them, he will be faithful to forgive us every time. God is just to forgive us our sins because of Christ, and he will continue to cleanse us from all unrighteousness."

The believer confesses the sin, repents of it, receives God's forgiveness, and moves on. Your record is "cleared of guilt" ... "All [your] guilt is gone" at that point, according to David. You may have committed the "crime," but God deems you innocent! What kind of crazy love is that! But we know from experience that life tends to be more complicated than that much of the time. We don't always *feel* that our "guilt is gone," even after we've followed the biblical prescription to deal with our shortcomings. Why is that such a challenge sometimes? We're going to get there in just a few pages but, before we do, we need to expand on two concepts that relate to true guilt first.

Widening the Lens on True Guilt—
Exactly What is "Repentance"?

In Christian circles we are frequently encouraged to "repent" when we've messed up in our relationship with God. But what does it mean for us to "repent," exactly? It can be a foggy notion. I'll start by saying what repentance is *not*. It's not remorse, which is sincerely feeling sorry about what you did or didn't do. The Gospel of Matthew tells us that Judas felt remorse after he betrayed Jesus, but he did not repent. Peter, on the other hand, also felt remorse after his betrayal of Jesus, but he did repent—and his relationship with Jesus was restored.

Repent literally means "to change your mind" about what you've done, that you understand it was wrong, and that you consciously choose not to do it again. But there is a fuller meaning to this term that believers need to appreciate. Repentance is really a turning—a *turning away from the sin* we've committed and an intentional *turning toward God*. For his guidance. For his strength. For his involvement in our decision-making. So, in a real sense, repentance is also a change in *how we think* about who God is and how he wants to engage us in life.

For example, let's go back to the issue of stealing, but let's consider a more adult context. Let's say you're a waitress at a five-star restaurant. Your salary is minimal, but you do fantastic when it comes to tips. (This is going to be a tough one for some people, but here goes!) It's tax time. Jesus said to "render to Caesar the things that are Caesar's, and to God the things that are God's" (Mark 12:17, NASB1995). Uncle Sam has regulations about tips. You are supposed to declare them and pay taxes on them. But you don't feel you can afford to declare your tips this year because, if you do—well, you're going to go "under." Besides, *nobody* declares their tips, right? Or, even if they do, they declare a miniscule amount. And who's going to find out, anyway? Wow. I know I'm not going to be popular on this one, but that is a form of stealing from the US government.

For sure, stealing is wrong, but hear this—*the greater wrong* is not grabbing on to the truth that God is your provider. That's one of his names in the Bible! You don't have to steal anything because His Word promises that "my God will supply all your needs according to His riches in glory in Christ Jesus" (Philippians 4:19, NASB1995).

Just as an example, then, your prayer of repentance might sound something like this: "Lord, stealing from Uncle Sam was wrong. I change my mind [I repent] about what I've done and will declare my tips in the future. I also repent about how I think about you. You are my provider. You will meet all my needs in Christ Jesus. I don't know how you're going to do it, but I trust you that you are going to work it out so I can pay my bills."

That's repentance! Listen—confessing our sin to God is really good, but it doesn't tell him anything he doesn't already know. Leaning into who almighty God is, who we are in him, and the inheritance we have in him, on the other hand, is a conscious act of faith that blesses him even more. It's changing our minds about the depth of our relationships with God and the level of trust we have that he will come through. It's an invitation to the Spirit to remind us that he can empower us to act in a godly way the next time around.[9]

Widening the Lens on True Guilt—Conviction Versus Condemnation

The second issue related to true guilt that causes confusion for believers is that of conviction versus condemnation. What's the difference? Godly guilt comes through the *conviction* of the Holy Spirit. In the Bible, "conviction" refers to a realization that you truly have done something wrong. It gently leads you to repentance. Condemnation, on the other hand, is part of Satan's arsenal. It is an accusation followed by a declaration that you are guilty, but it comes with a sentence, some punishment, attached to it. You must pay a price to atone for your wrongdoing. So, spiritually speaking, conviction and condemnation are not the same.

Here is the wonderful, good news we need to imprint in our brains and hearts—on a spiritual level, there is no condemnation for those who are in Christ Jesus (Romans 8:1). Let's put some flesh on this to help us understand where the cross comes into play on our behalf.

On the night he was betrayed, Jesus was bound and dragged before a mock court of the Jewish religious leaders collectively known as the Sanhedrin. They had determined beforehand that they needed to come up with some charge against him that was serious enough so they could sentence him to death. Because their strategy was not working well initially, the chief priest, Caiaphas, posed a direct question to Jesus, "Are you the Messiah, the Son of God?" Jesus fearlessly confessed that he was! There was no way the Sanhedrin was going to accept that. Matthew 26:62–66 (NLT) says, "Then the high priest tore his clothing to show his horror, shouting, 'Blasphemy! Why do we need other witnesses? You have all heard his blasphemy. What is your verdict?'

"'Guilty!' they shouted. 'He deserves to die!'"

Let us lay hold of the sheer love and grace of God here. Jesus was falsely pronounced "guilty" of sin ("blasphemy") so that you, as a believer in Christ, would never have that verdict pronounced against you for your sins! Jesus was condemned to death in an earthly court so that you would never be condemned to death in a heavenly one! Jesus died as the penalty of his condemnation so that you would never have to experience spiritual death as your penalty.

Jesus was truly our substitute in every way, all so that we could enjoy eternal life with him. Romans 8:1 (NASB) is thus a powerful verse to keep in your armor of truth: "Therefore there is now no condemnation at all to those who are in Christ Jesus!" After he confessed his affair to God, David wrote in Psalm 32:5 (NLT), "And you forgave me! All my guilt is gone." That is a profound declaration. In Christ Jesus, all our guilt is *gone*! You don't have to carry the burden of guilt for what you've done any longer.

Think of it this way: Jesus literally took the guilt from your hands when he went to the cross! Guilt, therefore, doesn't "belong" to you anymore. Jesus has freed you from the haunting of it! That is not to say that there won't be a civil punishment here on this earth for a serious crime. If you kill someone, you will likely be convicted and condemned to spend a long time in jail, but God can still forgive you for committing the offense, even if no one else on the earth does!

So, to keep it simple, conviction comes from the Holy Spirit. Its purpose is to open our eyes to the need to repent and to turn us back to the heart of Father-God and his will. It brings freedom in our relationship with God. Taking appropriate action when the Holy Spirit convicts us restores our sense of joy, peace, and intimacy with God. Recall that two names for the Holy Spirit are Counselor and Comforter. He counsels us when we have done something wrong, and then comforts us with the surety of forgiveness when we confess our poor choices to him. In that light, receiving the conviction of the Holy Spirit is really a recommitment to trusting God with a specific area of our lives.

Condemnation, on the other hand, comes from Satan himself. He emphasizes how guilty we are and that *we* should bear the penalty for our wrongs. With malicious slyness, he tries to tie us to our past failures and to negate the power of the cross. He strives to convince us that we must incur some punishment in addition to the cross for us to be worthy of God's forgiveness and acceptance! His aim, therefore, is to keep us trapped in ongoing cycles of self-condemnation. If he is successful, we often feel distance connecting to God because we're never totally sure that we've done enough to atone for our sins.

You may be saying to yourself, "Okay, Bill. I kind of know a lot of this stuff already—what you're saying about guilt, repentance, and conviction. And I know that God forgives me when I bring my sin to him. But why do I still *feel* guilty even after all that?"

Great question. That brings us to our next topic: *false* guilt.

Selah.

Reflections:

How has this section brought clarity to the issues of true guilt, repentance, conviction, and condemnation for you?

Has an ongoing feeling of guilt plagued you? Read and consider memorizing Romans 8:1. Say it aloud—multiple times if necessary. Let the power of the cross sink into your spirit to bring freedom from guilt.

False Guilt

True guilt was fairly straight forward, but the picture gets more muddled with false guilt; that's why we need to sort it out. False guilt comes in two general forms. The first is the obvious one implied in the actual phrase "false guilt"—that is, *guilt that has no basis in fact*. It is unwarranted guilt because you didn't do anything wrong! This type of false guilt is often meant to be manipulative, a way that someone tries to get you to do what he or she wants. We've all encountered this at some point. Here we go …

You've been working like a dog all week and are exhausted. You really need some down time. But then, you get a call. "Hey, Sandra. I know you've already put in your shift at the homeless shelter this week, but Brian had to cut out at the last minute, and we were hoping you might be able to fill in for him."

"Yeah. Thanks, Tina. Really appreciate your thinking of me, but I'm not going to be able to help out this time. I'm so sorry."

"You know, these people need you. When we volunteered for this ministry, we all understood there would be times when we would have to 'walk the extra mile.' We really could use your help, Sandra—especially since you don't live that far away. And you're so good with the clients. They *love* you!"

Uh-huh. You can see Sandra's arm getting twisted slowly but surely. Tina probably works undercover for the WWF (World Wrestling Federation)! Tina is trying to force Sandra into feeling guilty enough to change her mind in order to fill the empty shift. She is taking an aggressive posture by throwing a blanket of false guilt over Sandra. Along with the false guilt, Tina is showing us that she isn't honoring Sandra's boundaries or showing respect for her friend. It's totally okay for Sandra to say "no can do" and *not* feel guilty in the least!

The second type of false guilt relates to our inability to receive forgiveness from God, from others, or even from ourselves! Once we have identified our sins, confessed them, and repented as I discussed above, we are forgiven and free to move on. The love and grace of Jesus on the cross poured spiritual Clorox on our mistakes two thousand years ago. We are clean. We are forgiven! So, this type of false guilt is *the ongoing feeling of guilt even after we have confessed our sin to God or to others and repented.* We step into a prison of self-condemnation rather than experiencing the freedom that should follow repentance.

Here is a tremendous, counterintuitive revelation: when you've put your faith in Christ, your sin does not alter how God feels about you—at all! He loves you as much after you have sinned as he did before you sinned because he is total love. There is no variation in Total Love, Jesus. He is our rock-solid constant. Your relationship with him is still as secure after you mess up as it was beforehand. That's what true covenant relationship is all about. (I will discuss covenant in more detail in book three.)

Though your sin is not pleasing to God, *he does not reject you.* You may stumble, but you will not fall; you may sink, but you will not drown; you may fail, but you are not a failure. God's extravagant promise is that he will *never* leave you nor forsake you. "If [you] are unfaithful, he remains faithful, for he cannot deny who he is" (2 Timothy 2:13, NLT). However, what sin does do:

- If you don't acknowledge, confess, and deal with it, it opens a door for Satan to have inroads into your life, especially in that area where you compromised yourself.
- If you do confess your wrongdoing but have difficulty receiving God's forgiveness, it will make it harder for you to have *intimacy*

with Papa-God. Not on God's end, but on yours. That's what Satan wants, to disconnect you in any way he can from God.

This issue of holding on to guilt due to an inability to feel forgiven is a common stumbling block for many believers. It's yet another way the enemy imprisons us and tries to sabotage how God's grace can work in our lives. Satan packs his quiver with five very sharp, barbed arrows of false-guilt-lies. Let's explore these one by one so we have a greater awareness of the head games the adversary plays with us.

Satan's Five Arrows of False Guilt

━━━━◆━━━ The first arrow the enemy shoots is that God *can't* forgive you for a particular sin. Here are some of the lines that might get stuck on repeat in your mind:

> ➤ "What you did was *so* bad, there's *no way* God could forgive you for that."
> ➤ "You are an absolute failure! You will never measure up to God's standards. Don't even bother thinking that he will forgive you."
> ➤ "Wow! You so betrayed God's love for you on that one. You're like Judas on steroids!"
> ➤ "You were so totally aware that what you were doing was outrageously wrong, and you did it anyway. Talk about abusing God's grace. Sorry, loser; you know God doesn't tolerate that kind of garbage. Don't waste his time asking for forgiveness."

Recently, Jeanie was sharing the gospel with a young woman and invited her to put her faith in Christ. The young woman, Sabrina, was hesitant at first until Jeanie investigated her reluctance.

"Well," she responded, "I didn't think God would be interested in me because I used to sleep with my boyfriend."

Sabrina essentially believed that sleeping with her boyfriend was the "unpardonable sin." She continued to carry false guilt and shame even after acknowledging her wrong. Jeanie helped her receive God's forgiveness, and she accepted Jesus as her Lord and Savior at the same time. It was a tender, beautiful moment.

Right now, some of you might be thinking, "You know, I could deal with confessing sleeping with my significant other to God. But what I did was way, way worse than that. I just don't know if God could ever forgive me for what I did. I don't even believe I *should* be forgiven!"

You are not the only one who thinks like that. But for a minute, can we get down to it, really down? Let me ask you—what was it that was so bad that God "can't" forgive you? Maybe, like Kristen, you had an abortion, or perhaps even more than one. Or you brought your friend to a party one night and he overdosed. He just never woke up. Or maybe you were hoping that no one would ever find out that you cheated on your wife, but the torment of guilt and shame has shredded you ever since and you don't have a clue how to escape it. Or _____. You fill in the blank.

None of this is good. You know that, and I know that. These are what some would consider "unpardonable sins." People drag these heavy weights around with them day in and day out, sometimes for a lifetime. Maybe you are one of those people. What I'm saying is that you are falling for the lie of the adversary if you believe God *can't* forgive you.

Here's the truth. The cross is bigger and more powerful than your sin, whatever it might be. Jesus took every "guilty" hit that you and everyone else in the world could possibly imagine and nailed it to the cross. He is just beyond incredible. That is the grace he offers you right now. You don't have to *feel* worthy to believe that God will forgive you. The reality is that *none* of us could ever make ourselves worthy enough to receive God's forgiveness. We need a Savior. That's why he sent one. In Christ, we are accepted and acceptable. We are always the beloved of God, no matter what. He will never disown us. That's what grace is all about! Jesus makes us worthy to be forgiven because he already bore the punishment for our failures.

Let me encourage you if you believe you have committed the unpardonable sin. Don't let the enemy of your soul hold you in the shackles that God *can't* forgive you. It's a lie. You can let it go now. Really, he *wants* you to let it go. You don't need to hold the guilt in any longer. You don't need to keep hiding from him in fear. Our gracious Father-God has been waiting for you to come back for a long time. His love will wash you of your sin and wipe it from his hard drive. That's what the cross was for—to bring you back "home" to his heart.

It still amazes me to think about this, but Jesus took all our guilt away *two thousand years ago*! It's time for you to walk into freedom in Christ. Give it to him, and you will finally sense the release you have been yearning for, for so long. Remember Kristen? She was able to receive God's forgiveness and to forgive herself for the abortion. When she did, the overwhelming, supernatural peace of God descended upon her and, at long last, she could rest in the embrace of God's love.

So, if you need to be a Kristen right now, please take some time, maybe a lot of time, to lay the load of false guilt you've been carrying at the foot of the cross. That's where you will find the altar of the Father's kindness and grace. At that altar, Jesus gives you a sure promise that he will pull a trade with you: your burden for his rest (Matthew 11:28). It's over. "It is finished" are Jesus's greatest words of freedom to us.

Key Verses:

> Some of us once sat in darkness, living in the dark shadows
> of death. We were prisoners to our pain, chained to our
> regrets ... Then we cried out, "Lord, help us! Rescue us!"
> And he did! His light broke through the darkness and
> he led us out in freedom from death's dark shadow and

snapped every one of our chains" (Psalm 107:10, 13–14, TPT).

Then Jesus said, "Come to me, all of you who are weary and carry heavy burdens, and I will give you rest" (Matthew 11:28, NLT).

"I, even I, am he who blots out your transgressions, for my own sake, and remembers your sins no more" (Isaiah 43:25, NIV).

Selah. (Please take as much time as you need to process this first arrow.)

Satan's second arrow that keeps us stuck in false guilt is that God *won't* forgive us of our sin. Here's what this arrow "sounds" like:

➢ "You've had to confess that sin to God so many times; do you really think he believes you anymore?"
➢ "Why are you wasting God's time? He's so done with your excuses."
➢ "Really? You can't get more creative than that? Your apology for what you did sounds so lame. Remember, you're talking to the God of the universe!"

A friend of mine shared that she felt a compulsion to repent of the same sins "over and over and over again" because she wasn't sure God would forgive her. "God won't love me if I make the slightest mistake," was the way she worded it. Basically, she was pleading with God to forgive her and was afraid that he wouldn't unless she lived a perfect life. Talk about false guilt, not to mention the impossibility of leading a perfect life! We need to shut the enemy down immediately when he starts to take us there.

But there are big parentheses here too. This idea that God won't forgive us of our errors tends to take hold when we find ourselves falling into the same sin repeatedly. We get so discouraged that we begin to give up on ourselves. The weird thing that happens is that *we project our discouragement onto God!* That's when we may fall for the lie that God is so disappointed in us that he is giving up on us too—and *won't* forgive us of our faults anymore! It's a flat out lie!

However, if you do happen to find yourself in the situation where you are succumbing to the same sin repeatedly, I would suggest that you are not going deep enough to deal with the root issues of the problem. For instance, let's say you get drunk ... again! In fact, you are a closet alcoholic. You confess your drunkenness to God, repent of it, and express your desire to lean into his strength the next time temptation comes your way.

All of that is good and fine, but it's not nearly enough. You need to go deeper, much deeper into that cave. You might need to deal with the fact that your dad was an alcoholic and didn't provide for you well when you were a child. And then he divorced your mom for a younger woman, abandoning you both when you were twelve years old. In fact, you still hate him! If you don't work on the *root* problems, you will probably be repenting to God sometime soon for getting drunk yet again.

I hope this is all making sense. You *must* go deep if you truly want to experience God's victory and peace. Let this truth touch you—God can only take you as high as you're willing to go deep.

Arrow three in the adversary's quiver of false guilt can really mess with your head. You know you have fallen short, and you bring it to God. You repent and commit to approaching that situation differently in the future in the strength of Christ. You are able to receive his forgiveness but then, at some later time, *the enemy brings up the past and accuses you of that same old mistake again, and again, and again.* Understand that one of Satan's names is "the accuser" (Revelation 12:10).

The accuser's attack is so relentless that you question whether it is Satan or God speaking to you! You begin to doubt that you were genuine when you confessed your fault, and therefore wonder if God truly forgave you. You focus so much on your past sins that you forget you've already been wholly, totally, and forever forgiven of them! Essentially, what the adversary is doing is resurrecting the misdeeds of the past to entrench you in the guilt of the past, all with the goal of making you feel disqualified from your future in Christ. That's literally the line the devil will whisper to you repeatedly, "What you did disqualifies you from all the good God had for you!"

All of this is Satan's variation of the condemnation theme. The emphasis with these recurring accusations is to cast doubt on the fact that you were forgiven. But if you were sincere when you repented, the guilt is gone. By faith, the guilt is gone. You can rest in the assurance of God's forgiveness.

Just like with condemnation, anytime you feel accused, know that it's a barb from the enemy.

Selah.

Arrow number four that Satan will hurl at us is the *false guilt imposed on us by another*. The other person's purpose in this is to manipulate you or to put you down out of his own insecurity, as I mentioned earlier. It's a way of controlling you or perhaps making you feel bad as a form of vengeance. In relationships, the classic lead-in line for this is, "If you really loved me, you would _____."

I remember a Sunday back when I was in the first grade. Our family was very consistent about attending Sunday services, but one Sunday morning, I didn't feel so well and stayed home. Later that day I felt better, so I went outside to play. My older brother strutted out to the back yard and, let me tell you, *his* quiver was full that day!

"So, look who got better so quick! You know it's a sin to lie about being

25

sick. You know it's a mortal sin if you missed church on purpose. You could even go to hell right now if you died!"

Aren't big brothers wonderful? Talk about a guilt trip! As a little kid, I almost wet my pants. I was petrified to tears. It took me about two seconds to "repent" so I didn't go to hell, and that was the last time I missed church as a kid too!

But let's go to real-time here for those of you who do attend church. If you commit yourself to a certain church "family," at some point, you need to act like you're part of the family and help out, to serve in some capacity. That's not meant to guilt you in any way; it's just what family is supposed to do. Help each other. Pull for each other. Sacrifice for each other. Having said that, I also need to point out that "stuff happens" in church sometimes just like it does in the world, and that includes false guilt (and shame) imposed on you by a brother or sister in Christ.

Jeanie and I know a woman who has an amazing heart for God, is incredibly generous with her time and finances, and has a gift for loving people into the kingdom. Unfortunately, she overdid it for an extended period of time and just burnt out. I mean, *really burnt out*. I don't know if you've ever encountered someone like that. Speaking from a medical perspective now, it's difficult for burnt-out people to do even routine, simple, every-day functions for themselves, never mind try to continue their usual commitments to others. It's like being turbo-depressed, like walking through water all day every day. So, our friend pulled way back and stopped serving at the church. That's not what she wanted to do; it's what she *had* to do for her own health and well-being.

A church team leader who didn't really understand what was going on became stern with our friend on more than one occasion when she saw her at church. She told our friend that it was time to come back from "vacation" and help again. Then, one Sunday when the pastor was encouraging people to serve, this leader looked directly at our friend and nodded, as if to say, "See? Even Pastor is trying to tell you that you need to get back to business!"

This ministry leader was unwittingly putting a false guilt trip and laying shame on our friend. It was horrible, exactly what our friend did *not* need at the time. That was *condemnation*, not conviction. It was not healthy, compassionate, or godly.

Selah.

Reflections:

There's so much here in these four arrows that we've discussed so far. Have you ever felt that God couldn't or wouldn't forgive you for some past wrong you committed? Do you now see how those thoughts were from the enemy? He was out to steal your peace and disrupt your connection with God.

Think of a time when someone persuaded you to do something you really didn't feel was the right thing to do. Were you able to recognize what was happening? How did it make you feel? How did you respond? How did it impact your relationship with that person going forward? Would you respond differently now?

━━━◆ The fifth and final arrow in Satan's quiver of false guilt is even more subtle—it is *the false guilt we impose upon ourselves*, either consciously or subconsciously. As a pediatrician, I can tell you, this type of guilt is highly damaging, especially to the heart of a child.

A typical example I encountered in my practice would be a child whose parents were getting divorced. Even when the divorce had absolutely nothing to do with the child, the youngster invariably believed that he or she was the cause of the break-up. The child usually thought he or she was just plain bad or had done something to cause the parents to fight, and now they were going to break up. Sometimes it would be extremely difficult, even impossible, for the child's own parents to persuade him or her that the separation was simply not the child's fault.

As one who attended to the health-care needs of children and young adults, I must also touch on child abuse here because *any form of abuse* (verbal, physical, or sexual) invariably creates self-induced false guilt and shame. In his or her innocence, a child often comes to believe that he or she *must* have done something wrong to *deserve* the abuse. Why else would a "trustworthy" adult act toward him or her in that way if it weren't so? In this immature way of thinking, the helpless child-victim concludes that the perpetrator's actions or words *must* have been justified. With sexual abuse, the situation becomes more complicated. The victim may be unwilling to tell anyone what happened for fear he or she will not be believed or fear of the consequences to him- or herself or to other family members. It is truly sinister.

If you are a victim of abuse of whatever type and you know deep down that you have not fully processed the pain of it, I would like to ask you to please find a quiet spot where you can be alone with God right now, where no one can hear you, and you have no time constraints. We are going to do an "activation," where we invite the Holy Spirit into the moment to do a work of healing in your heart for whatever abuse you endured.

If you are not ready to undertake this step, please do not feel obligated to do so. Or, if this situation does not apply to you, simply bypass this section and continue on to the "key verses" below. There will be more opportunities in *Deep Calling to Deep* to revisit the trauma and heartache of the past.

God is kind in all his ways. He will never force you to do anything you are not ready for. But understand that it is unquestionably his will that you are healed of what caused you so much angst. It is also his will that you not bear the guilt for the abuse that happened to you any longer.

Activation:

Now that you have found a quiet, private spot, ask the Holy Spirit to join you as you return to the event that devastated you. Please understand, you should not try to do this "alone." You need the strength, wisdom, and guidance of the Spirit in this process. Using your own words, please invite the Holy Spirit into the moment out loud and wait patiently.

As the Spirit rekindles old memories and past wounds are reopened, begin to say to yourself *out loud again*, "It was not my fault. It was not my fault. It was not my fault." Repeat it over and over and over again—as many times as you need to and as long as you need to, as quietly or as loudly as you need to. Until it sinks in, until it shakes you to the core, and until you sense that your words are not your own anymore but are melding with the echoes of heaven coming from the very throne of God himself ... and you actually believe, perhaps for the first time, "It was not my fault."

Now, in a sacred release, imagine yourself under a waterfall. See the water flowing over you from the top of your head down to your feet. It is the Holy Spirit cleansing you, restoring your purity, washing away the guilt, shame, and the false responsibility you have borne for the abuse. Receive your cleansing. Bask in the presence of the Father as he pours his love out on you. Stay there until you truly sense that you are innocent, that you are free, and that you are whole in that area again.

Please take as much time as necessary. If you need to "call it a day" at this juncture instead of reading on, do so. Follow the leading of the Spirit as he applies a healing salve to your heart.

Selah. (Again, please take as much time as you need. Do not rush the process.)

Now you have a better picture of just how evil the devil can be when you are vulnerable. Satan uses these five arrows of trash-lies to drag you into false guilt so that you condemn yourself. The lies keep you spinning the wheels of remorse and regret. You get so bogged down with how bad you feel or how angry you believe God is with you that you are reluctant to reach out to him to seek forgiveness and healing. You don't feel worthy of his love or forgiveness, and that is exactly Satan's ploy.

Here is God's take on all of this: "And I am convinced that nothing can ever separate us from God's love. Neither death nor life, neither angels nor demons, neither our fears for today nor our worries about tomorrow—not even the powers of hell can separate us from God's love" (Romans 8:38, NLT). This is such a potent verse. Jesus paid the price. He took it all from you on the cross two thousand years ago. You are free from the guilt and free from the false guilt of your misdeeds of the past. You are free.

Key Verses:

> Let us go right into the presence of God with sincere hearts fully trusting him. For our guilty consciences have been sprinkled with Christ's blood to make us clean, and our bodies have been washed with pure water. (Hebrews 10:22, NLT)

> He will cover you with his feathers. He will shelter you with his wings. His faithful promises are your armor and protection. Do not be afraid of the terrors of the night, nor

the arrow that flies in the day … Though a thousand fall at your side, though ten thousand are dying around you, these evils will not touch you. (Psalm 91:4–5, 7, NLT)

Selah.

Reflections:

Which of these arrows of false guilt have you struggled with the most? Why do you think it's been so hard?

Take some time and ask the Holy Spirit to guide you back to any other memories of false guilt. Ask him to meet you there and to cleanse you from it. Forgiveness may also be needed as you reminisce. Again, if that is too difficult for you right now, jot down some notes about those personal circumstances. We will explore the topic of victory in the battles to forgive in book two.

The Shame Game

Now that we understand guilt and false guilt well, we are ready to take on the real demon lurking in the far reaches of this cave, shame. We already know that true guilt and false guilt are often tied to shame, but we rarely separate them when we talk about how we feel. "I feel so much guilt and shame," we say, as if they are one and the same. So, what exactly is the difference? Here it is.

Whereas guilt and false guilt relate to *what we do*, shame is about *who we are*. That merits repeating. Guilt and false guilt deal with what we say, how we think, or how we act. Shame is about who we believe ourselves to be. If we want to frame this distinction in psychological jargon, guilt and false guilt deal with *behavior*. Shame is about *identity*. Remember, one of the things the enemy seeks to "steal, kill, and destroy" is our identity.

You do something wrong or *think* you've done something wrong, or perhaps something was done to you as an innocent victim. You feel shame. Shame is what persuades you that you are a bad person for what happened, that you will never measure up, that you are beyond hope, a good-for-nothing, a nobody, a whatever.

Everyone has to deal with shame. Many live in shame as a way of life. It often begins early on with a few choice labels tossed your way as a child. The disparaging words may come from parents, siblings, friends, teachers, coaches, employers, and occasionally, even pastors. Then we echo those labels to ourselves over and over and over again. Shame revolves around the negative "I am" statements we make to ourselves. "Are you kidding me?

Why did I do that? Yeah, I'm just really dumb. Mom was totally right on that one. A real dumbo."

See the "I am" there? "*I am* just really dumb." Remember, "death and life are in the power of the tongue," even when that tongue is speaking it out in the depths of our own minds (Proverbs 18:21, NASB1995). Every time those derogatory labels resonate within us, we are "speaking" death to ourselves; we are letting Satan steal part of who God created us to be. Our true identity in Jesus ebbs away a little bit at a time. Ultimately, what shame comes down to is a personal sense of unworthiness of the love and attention of others. Here are some of the lines we recite to ourselves to reinforce our sense of unworthiness, the kind of falsehoods the enemy wants to sear into our beings:

➤ "No one really cares about me or what I have to say."
➤ "I don't really matter."
➤ "No one would really notice or miss me if I decided not to show up anymore."
➤ "My presence doesn't really make much of a difference in the world."

In other words, when shame overcomes you, you *internalize* the label that was declared over you (or that you conjured up for yourself) by attaching it to your identity. It's at this point that the wrong morphs from what you've done into who you are—a nobody, a person who is not worth knowing or getting to know, an absolute failure as a human being. It makes you feel unwanted, undesirable, and the one who is not "chosen" by others. That's a perfect definition of shame—an ongoing sense that you are the "unchosen," the "never-enough" person on the planet.

When you are totally steeped in shame, it's like you don't know how to swim and you're in water over your head. You are kicking, your arms are flailing, and you're doing anything you can for a gasp of air, but then you go right back down. It's living a slow death. Yet, that's the whirlpool where multitudes writhe for a breath of significance each and every day. The bottom line is this: shame robs you of your personal sense of worth and distorts your personal reality. You come to believe horrible lies about yourself because shame is always rooted in lies.

Where is Satan taking you when he unloads this dump of shame on you? Simple. He's the master disconnector. His goal is to pull you away from God and away from others. He uses the deceitfulness of shame to keep you from pursuing God because you believe you are not worthy of the Father's love or forgiveness. If you don't believe that God loves you or that he will forgive you, you won't be able to love or forgive yourself easily either. That is precisely how shame evolves into a lifestyle of self-rejection.

The end result is that, to one extent or another, you remain mired in the mud of shame, tied to past wrongs, isolated from God, disconnected from others, and unable to make long-term, meaningful forward progress in life. It's like riding one of those brilliantly painted horses on a carousel at the carnival. The horse takes you up and down, up and down. You're in constant motion, and, at times, it can even be exhilarating. But you're not really getting anywhere; you're just swirling around in circles. You're not "galloping" off into who you were created to be, into your true identity in Christ.

As if all of that is not enough, a kind of grief sets in. Jeanie had a great insight on this: "The grief comes because you are lamenting the loss of your own worth and value. That leads you to feel a constant need to look for identity and affirmation from other people." Shame and grief combined are a tremendous double-burden. They bring you down and wear you out—physically, emotionally, and spiritually.

The medical tie-in here also has tremendous implications. In your body, shame triggers a reaction in the nervous system similar to how you respond to danger. It's called the fight-or-flight response. Stress hormones kick in big time, causing you to want to run, to get away, to disappear, or, less commonly with shame, to fight.

The collateral psychological damage from shame is also striking. There is no question that shame is linked to depression, anxiety, and often to relational difficulties. The spin-offs from those are numerous as well, leading to various addictions: substance abuse, alcoholism, promiscuity, and possibly suicide. The damage offshoots may also show up in ways you may not be aware of, such as rage attacks, perfectionism, the inability to say no to others (i.e., difficulty with setting boundaries), a tendency to be critical of yourself, or to feel like you're always on the edge of doing something wrong. Shame creates a constant tension within, like a rubber band within the psyche that is always taut.

Perhaps one of the most vicious aspects of the spirit of shame (and there is a spiritual aspect to it) is that shame weaves its way into the soul to become a self-fulfilling prophecy. What I mean by that is that the leaven of shame can sometimes become so kneaded into our identity and so familiar to us that the good things in life (love, joy, peace, patience, kindness, etc.) seem foreign and therefore uncomfortable to us. We don't believe we deserve to have good things. So, what do we do? *We self-sabotage* the good things that actually do come our way. We behave in ways that will bolster shame because that's what we're used to feeling; that's what feels "right."

The thinking goes something like this: consciously, I believe "I am bad." The subconscious parenthesis is, "So I will do bad things that will confirm that I really am bad." We act out. We do the passive-aggressive thing. We get into arguments over silly things with people we care about. We lie. We steal. Whatever. We behave poorly because we believe that is who we are. "I am bad"; therefore, I do bad things because it's true!

A young woman we mentor recently shared how she is contending with this self-sabotaging as it pertains to her own battle with anxiety. Here's how she expressed it: "Experiencing the peace of God is so new and different for me that it feels bad and scary! So, I go back to my old anxiety because I feel more comfortable there … and then I feel guilty and ashamed for doing that. Like Paul says, 'I do the thing that I hate!'" But she is getting to a place of deeper healing and trusting God so that she can recognize the schemes of the enemy. It is getting easier and easier for her to fight back and say, "No! You are not taking me back to that old way!"

Do you see how detrimental this self-sabotaging is, though? Satan aims to take us out, render us a nonentity, people who will pose no threat to him and who will feel far from God. So, he invites us to the constant pity party of shame, and we are the only ones attending. That's why I call it one of the demons within.

Earlier, I mentioned Adam and Eve's response after they felt shame in the garden of Eden; they tied fig leaves around their waists and tried to play hide-and-seek with God behind a tree. Now, ask yourself, "What were they thinking when they decided they could physically hide from the God of the universe?" That's exactly the point: they were *not* thinking!

Shame and all the other demons we will discuss in this trilogy *alter the way we think*. They twist our perceptions of life and of reality. Unfortunately, when we don't think clearly, we make poor, destructive decisions. That poor decision-making may carry over to how we relate to God, how we comprehend what is happening (or not happening!) to us, what we hear in the comments people make to us, how we see ourselves, and—this one is *big*: how we relate to others. Shame is one of the reasons, for instance, that victims of domestic abuse continue to tolerate the violence. Because they have lost all sense of self-worth, the truth of their ill-treatment is totally torqued in their minds. They don't recognize it as a problem and therefore stay in those dysfunctional relationships because they don't believe they deserve any better.

In short, shame impacts *everything* in our lives.

Selah.

Reflections:

There was a lot packed into these last few pages. Consider re-reading them to draw out the main points. You might want to transfer some of the thoughts that really stuck out to you into your journal.

Now that you have a better grasp of shame … do you believe you are carrying any shame now? What are you ashamed of? Take time to journal some of the things from the past that have caused you to feel shame. Put them aside for the time being until we get through how to address them.

There's no time limit here. You may start with one or two things, but those two may trigger other memories. Invite the Holy Spirit to show you the shame-hurts of the past.

The Deep of Shame—Going to Its Core

Some ten years ago Dr. Brené Brown, a PhD in social work, started a research project with the intention of learning more about people's attitudes concerning how they connected to others. It only took six weeks before she hit a wall. She would ask questions about love, belonging, and connection, but would frequently get responses from people about their heartbreaks, isolation, and disconnection instead.

These unexpected replies threw her. She had to figure out what was going on, and she did. Dr. Brown eventually determined that those in the survey who responded with those paradoxical, negative comebacks were struggling with *shame*. Here's what she said during a TED Talk: "And shame is really understood as the fear of disconnection—is there something about me that, if other people know it or see it, that I won't be worthy of connection? ... In order for connection to happen, we have to allow ourselves to be seen, really seen."[10] Boom!

When Adam and Eve hid themselves because they realized they were "naked" (Genesis 3:7), it wasn't so much about shame related to their physical bodies because they were just as naked before the Fall as they were after the Fall (see Genesis 2:25)! Their failure pricked their consciences; it opened a floodgate in their hearts that overwhelmed them. It shouted to them that things were drastically different in their relationship with their Creator. Their perception of themselves had changed because their evil desires had been "exposed." The two no longer wanted "to allow [themselves] to be seen, really seen." But, as Dr. Brown articulated so eloquently, when we hide behind whatever "fig leaves" we choose to hide behind so that we are not seen—we lose connection.

Adam and Eve had never experienced any spiritual distance from their Maker before, and the apprehension of it repulsed them. So, what did they do? They pulled back; they hid, just like we do. "Fight-or-flight," right? We bolt. We want to disappear. But Adam and Eve's reaction, to run and hide because of their shame, was exactly the wrong one. It seems paradoxical, but when we choose to bare our hearts, to be vulnerable and authentic with each other in the deep, hidden places of our being—those are the moments we forge our *closest* ties with one another. Those are the priceless opportunities for intimacy, soul to soul. That kind of transparency actually *builds* relationship. It's the same in our relationship with God. Shame, on the other hand, clamors at us that transparency will destroy connection—that we will be ridiculed or rejected again when we choose to share what is most meaningful to us or that what we have to share is not worth another person's time or attention.

The greatest loss for the original couple in the Fall, then, was that they had violated that profound, sweet, precious tie they had to the heart of God. In their spirits, they were immediately aware that they had lost their purity of relationship with him, so they concocted the fig-leaves idea to cover their blunder. But a human-made means of trying to cover sin would never work with God. He knows everything already anyway. Why not just be honest with him?

Dr. Brown continued with several other keen insights from her research. In addition to those who tended to view life negatively, there was another group of people who lived life much more positively. What distinguished those who had an upbeat outlook on life versus those with the negative bent? The doctor found that those with the optimistic approach had a strong sense of love and belonging and that they believed they were *worthy* of love and belonging. They were people of great courage: courage to be imperfect, courage to be authentic in recognizing their imperfection, and a willingness to be vulnerable with others about it.

Dr. Brown herself exemplified exactly what she was sharing at this TED Talk when she openly revealed her own personal striving with being vulnerable at the end of her presentation. She realized her own need to see a therapist to help her unpack her own shame! In this process, she came to a most beautiful conclusion: "And I know that vulnerability is the core of shame and fear and our struggle for worthiness, but it appears that it's also the birthplace of joy, of creativity, of belonging, of love."[11] Said so well.

Selah.

Reflections:

Do you agree with Dr. Brown that "shame is really understood as the fear of disconnection—is there something about me that, if other people know it or see it, that I won't be worthy of connection?"

If you have endured the deep pain of disconnection with others, ask the Holy Spirit to reveal if you played any part in how the disconnection developed. Write down your thoughts.

How We Overcome Shame

Shame, then, is part of the curse on humanity that came with the Fall in the garden of Eden. It was incorporated into the spiritual DNA of humankind at the very moment Adam and Eve bit into the forbidden fruit. Everyone experiences it. How do we deal with it? By quick way of review: true guilt we confess, repent, receive God's forgiveness, forgive ourselves, and move on. False guilt we release, recognizing the lies of Satan's arrows, and realizing we are truly forgiven.

Shame, however, we must intentionally confront because shame fastens its teeth into identity. If we take a passive approach, it will slowly bleed us of inspiration and joy in the Lord, imprison us in insignificance, and short-circuit God's purposes in our lives. Not only that, shame binds us up in our relationships with others. So, how do we become courageous enough to go deep? How do we become strong? How do we conquer? How do we disempower the spirit of shame so that we can become who we were meant to be in Christ?

The psychological world has its own answers to these questions, such as: you can heal yourself through self-forgiveness or self-compassion; you can resolve to change your behavior; you can take comfort in the fact that you are not the only one in the shame war. "Other human beings make mistakes too—we are all fallible, and that's okay." You can even "earn" your forgiveness and get rid of your shame by apologizing to the one you offended. Perhaps as a last resort, you can ask your "higher power" to forgive you.

These types of methods certainly may be helpful for some, but I must tell you from both a medical and a pastoral perspective, I don't believe the success rate is high, at least not in those I have ministered to. As a believer in Jesus, I would like to offer more substantial, effective alternatives.

Dealing with Shame—Step Number One: Be Brutally Transparent and Honest …

Be candid with yourself, with God, and possibly with others—about who you are and who you are not. That's the first step. Remember Dr. Brown's words, "Vulnerability is the core of shame …" You have to make that conscious choice to be transparent. It's not easy. Vulnerability involves humbling yourself. It requires great courage and trust to ask the Holy Spirit to reveal "the dark" in this cavern of shame within.

Let's look at some questions to help you process shame. As you sift through these questions, though, please be intentional. Go through the process slowly. If you were about to undergo anesthesia in an operating room, you would never instruct the surgeon to perform the surgery as quickly as she could. Meaningful interactions with the Great Physician always take time. Also, strongly consider journaling your thoughts, memories, and what the Spirit reveals to you. Leave space between sections of memories as the Lord may give you more clarity later about certain events or people.

So, when did the shame start? What was it that made you feel bad about yourself or left out (disconnected from others) or not enough? Was there a specific event that set it into motion? Was there a certain person involved? What lie was planted in your heart at that time? How has the lie taken root and impacted your life? What other later events added to that sense of shame?

Here's another angle to consider in your exploration of shame. Can you identify recurrent, negative patterns of behavior in your life—either in your own behavior or in how others have treated you? Do you think these recurrent negative patterns could be linked to shame in some way? How? As an example, because those plagued with shame always have poor self-esteem, they are natural targets for others to take advantage of them in some way.

So many never arrive at this step of confronting their shame. It's like the alcoholic who cannot admit to himself that he has a problem. He buries it. If you don't believe you have a problem with shame or you suppress it, you will never process it. If you never process it, you will never overcome the negative effect shame has on your life. It's that simple. That principle applies to each of the dragons you will face in our journey. Denial of our shortcomings is always destructive in one way or another. Realizing that you actually do have a problem with shame is a significant first step.

Selah.

Dealing with Shame—Step Number Two: Confessing to God

If your shame results from your own personal mistakes or failures, this part of dealing with shame is similar to dealing with guilt …

- Confess that you have fallen short and how you have harmed yourself through your sin.
- Confess that you have partnered with a lie(s) about yourself—and repent of that as well as of the actual sin itself.
- Confess that you need him. You need a Savior, Jesus, to help you get back on track.

My friend, Miguel, has a compelling testimony about how his life turned around after he mustered enough fortitude to face the truth about himself and worked it out with God. Miguel had committed his life to Christ at the age of eight, but became rebellious during his teen years. His own words are more potent than any paraphrase I could put together, so I will simply quote the email he sent me one day:

> At age fifteen, I rebelled against my mother and God. I got involved in the world of heavy metal and embraced Satan as my new god. In my mind, God had failed me. I was in so much pain that I used devil worshiping, entertainment, and music as a way of filling the void in my life. The more movies I saw, the deeper the void grew in my heart. I had also become sexually active trying to relieve the pain. Little did I know that it was causing me more pain and shame. I felt sad, condemned, depressed, and empty. Life was not worth living. At this point in my life, I knew I needed Christ, but I felt too ashamed to reach out to God. Certainly, God didn't want or need me. I was no good.
>
> That's when I recommitted my life to Christ. My girlfriend and now wife had just recently come to know Jesus. She suggested I read a book about knowing him. Half-way through the book, I began to cry, and I saw this bright light. I remember feeling so ashamed. All I could say was, "Please forgive me, Lord. Change my heart."
>
> I cannot begin to tell you the difference God has made in my life. <u>I know that God has forgiven my sins and given me a fresh start</u>. Before Christ, I was a loner, but now I have a church family and authentic friendships. I also have a sense of purpose, meaning, peace, hope, and love for others and especially myself. I wish I could say that my life is perfect, but it's not. God is still molding me into his own image.

44

I have great admiration for Miguel. He was willing to be brutally honest with himself and bring it humbly before the Lord. What a beautiful transformation has taken place since.

Selah.

Dealing with Shame—Step Number Three:
Shame Because of Your Sin Against Others

As far as the shame you hold for what you have done to others, James 5:16 (TPT) offers sound advice: "Confess and acknowledge how you have offended one another and then pray for one another to be instantly healed, for tremendous power is released through the passionate, heartfelt prayer of a godly believer!"

Confession and taking responsibility for our actions are so powerful in the spirit realm. It comes right back to being vulnerable again. Yet, we are often afraid to do it because we are embarrassed or may believe, "If I try to make it right, I might make it even worse!" Many times, that approach is not true; it's just another lie from the enemy. Look at James 5:16 again. It tells us that vulnerability opens the way to healing in the relationship. Additionally, you should try to remedy the harm committed, if that is possible. That lends credence to the sincerity of your apology and is the right thing to do.

There may be times, however, when you should really tune in to the guidance of the Spirit about how you should proceed. Confessing your sin to another may not be possible or may not even be wise. The one you hurt may have died. Perhaps you are ashamed of certain *thoughts* you had about another person, but that person is completely unaware of those sentiments. Sharing those thoughts may cause damage to the relationship that didn't even exist previously! Or perhaps there is a concern that the one insulted could respond violently. In such cases, you have to leave it at the cross and trust that God can handle the situation in his own way … but you can still experience freedom from the shame.

Selah.

Dealing with Shame—Step Number Four: Receive God's Forgiveness and Forgive Yourself

Intellectually, we understand that God forgives us when we confess our sins to him, but it can be really hard for us to receive his forgiveness. Why? Mostly because we have trouble forgiving ourselves. We wonder, "*Why* can't I forgive myself?" or "*Why* do I feel I am not worthy to be forgiven?"

Having difficulty breaking free from guilt and shame may relate to the fact that you are still living in an "Old Testament mindset": "An eye for an eye; a tooth for a tooth." In other words, you believe you need to suffer, that there must be some kind of payback or penance you must endure because of your mistakes to atone for your sins. In that way, so the thinking goes, you are showing God that you have learned from your wrongdoing and have paid an appropriate price for your misdeed so that he can deem you worthy of his love again.

We think that way because that's the way our world does it! You may get shamed in front of coworkers when your suggestion at the office did not work and cost the company a bundle; your girlfriend keeps unloading on you even after you apologize multiple times for your bad attitude; the basketball team ignores you after you miss an easy shot on what would have been a buzzer-beater. The lie is this, "When you mess up, you must be punished." Unfortunately, this Old Testament verdict doesn't relieve you of shame. It actually compounds it because you're never sure you've suffered enough for your failure!

But remember, that's not how it is for you in the new covenant relationship you have with Father-God in Christ. Through the shed blood of Jesus, your spirit is totally clean before God. Listen, if you don't believe

God loves you enough to forgive you of your sins, you won't be able to forgive yourself. *But*, if God does love you enough to forgive you, who are you not to forgive yourself? Are you so bold to consider that you are somehow a more just judge than God?

Let me restate that in a different way that packs a punch: not forgiving yourself is a form of idolatry—of placing your thoughts, beliefs, and feelings about yourself *higher than God's* and making a judgment against yourself that you are not worthy of forgiveness. God has declared you worthy of forgiveness because of the cross! To dismiss his grace is arrogant insanity. Not forgiving yourself may sound humble, but you know what that kind of thinking does? It says, "Jesus wasn't enough for me. The cross just wasn't enough." That warped thought process will sentence you to a prison of misery and depression for as long as you let it.

So, how do we forgive ourselves? Faith comes by hearing the truths from the Word of God worked into the fabric of the soul. Declare the scriptural promises of God out loud. Daily! For example, consider Isaiah 43:25 (NLT) and personalize it: "God—yes God alone, will blot out my sins for his own sake and will never think of them again." Speak that verse over yourself day after day until it really penetrates. It may take months, but persevere!

After dealing with God about your sin, ask him to give you a deeper revelation of his love for you. Receive his forgiveness by verbally thanking him for the grace and mercy of the cross. You might consider doing something as a prophetic, symbolic act—like cupping your hands and tossing your sin, guilt, and shame toward heaven like you would release a bird into the air—or writing about it on paper, tying it to a rock, and throwing it in a lake. I remember one time writing things down on a piece of paper and burning it in our wood-burning stove, sending it up to God in smoke, so to speak.

We do not need to succumb to the lies that we are not worthy of his love, not worthy to be forgiven, or not worthy of his great plans for our lives. In Christ, our spiritual DNA has been altered! Guilt and shame no longer have a "right" to have a hook in us. It is *not* who we are! We need to be aggressive about internalizing the truth of God's Word and his promises and meditating on those words so that they sink in deep. The truth of His Word is powerful—so much better than internalizing the shame!

He is a good God! The promises in His Word are bank. Go on a verse declaration rampage; run into the freedom of Christ as you were meant to!

> The Spirit who lives in you is greater than the spirit who lives in the world. (1 John 4:4, NLT)

> But in the depths of my heart I truly know that you, Yahweh, have become my Shield; You take me and surround me with yourself. Your glory covers me continually. You lift high my head when I bow low in shame. (Psalms 3:3, TPT)

> So now the case is closed. There remains no accusing voice of condemnation against those who are joined in life-union with Jesus, the Anointed One. (Romans 8:1, TPT)

Selah.

Reflections:

Any one of these first four steps of dealing with shame can be difficult. Which is the toughest for you: being brutally honest with yourself, confessing your failings to God, humbling yourself before others, or receiving God's love and forgiveness? Why do you think that step is the most challenging?

The path to freedom involves battles, confronting the lies of the enemy and the lies of your old mindset. Don't be discouraged if you are not totally successful with some of these steps just yet. The enemy uses discouragement to pull you away from God and to draw your focus away from pursuing freedom in Jesus. Keep moving forward, even if it seems like it's at a snail's pace for you.

Dealing with Shame—Step Number
Five: Confronting "God-Shame"

"God-shame"? What's that? Up to this point, we've spoken about dealing with our own shame. The truth of the matter, however, is that we frequently feel *God* is ashamed of us at the same time. That's right where the adversary wants us. Just like Adam and Eve in the garden of Eden, the enemy howls with laughter when we pull back and cover ourselves with whatever version of "fig leaves" we come up with. We fall for Satan's ruse that God is so disappointed in and so ashamed of us that we shouldn't dare consider going to him with our stuff—that he is going to reject us because we are no longer worthy of his love. That's exactly what Miguel shared in his testimony. This expectation of rejection is totally wrapped up in the false guilt ideas we spoke of earlier.

The other way God-shame shows up is when there is no apparent answer to prayer. Here are some of the darts the enemy whips at your brain:

➢ I must've *done* something wrong for God not to hear me.

➢ There must be something wrong *with me* that I just can't figure out.

➢ Maybe I'm just not doing enough for God.

➢ You know, I must not deserve what I'm praying for.

You know you're not in a good place when you question the promises of the Bible so that you say, "It just must not be God's will for _____," when it clearly is his will.

The two big situations where these lies creep in concern finding a mate (especially if the years are rolling on or if you're divorced) and getting pregnant. Shame is huge for people in these situations. Jeanie and I understand it well—we had trouble conceiving for years. When you're there, it's so easy to surrender to the conviction that "it must not be God's will for me to be married" or "I probably wouldn't be a good mom anyway." They provide a "reasonable" excuse for us to be able to handle why things aren't happening the way we would like. But, with rare exceptions, they are lies.

In Christ Jesus, you are totally acceptable and loved by Father-God. I can't offer you a simple reason for why your desire to be married or pregnant is not happening for you just yet, although God is highly intentional about his timing. But, it has nothing to do with him being disappointed or ashamed of you so that you don't "deserve" good things from God. In Christ, you are his beloved. Always. No one else could make you more pleasing or valuable to the Father than Jesus. Jesus paid the ultimate price so that you would have an abundant life in this life as well as in the afterlife (John 10:10).

Say *no* to the lies. Having children and being married are God's will for the overwhelming majority of men and women. Don't give up hope. Keep seeking him with confidence and expectation. Praise him and thank him in advance for what he will do, even when you don't feel like it. He is a good, good Daddy.

Key Verses:

> But seek first His kingdom and His righteousness and all these things will be added to you. (Matthew 6:33, NASB1995)

> If you then, being evil, know how to give good gifts to your children, how much more will your Father who is in heaven give what is good to those who ask Him! (Matthew 7:11, NASB1995)

Selah.

Dealing with Shame—Step Number Six:
Navigating the "Other" Kind of Shame

We have discussed being vulnerable in our relationships with God, with others, forgiving ourselves, and God-shame. But what about the shame that clings to us when others have victimized us? How do we deal with that?

It would be wonderful if every perpetrator:

- would admit he had wronged us,
- would acknowledge the hurt and pain he caused,
- would sincerely apologize,
- and would either try to rectify the situation or otherwise take responsibility for his actions in a just manner.

That type of response is really what most victims seek more than anything else. A mature approach after hurting someone restores some sense of dignity to the person who was mistreated. It validates that what happened was terribly wrong and provides some degree of justice for the evil committed. Unfortunately, in my professional and personal experience, that happens infrequently. Now what do we do?

Do you want to be released from the pain and the shame? Here's where the power of the Holy Spirit working in you as a believer flings the door wide open to freedom. What binds you to both the pain and the shame is *unforgiveness*. When you can forgive the person and can ask God to forgive him too, you sever the cord that holds you captive to the past event and to the pain. As long as you are chained to what is behind you, you cannot freely move ahead into all the good God has in store for you.

When you can believe that what happened was absolutely not your fault but arose from the perpetrator's own brokenness, then you are seeing the person as Jesus does. As you surrender it all to him, the Spirit empowers you to let go of the guilt and shame. You release the person from a debt he or she cannot pay, and you free yourself from the false responsibility for what happened.

This all makes forgiveness sound very easy. We know that's not true. There are a number of misconceptions that can hinder us from forgiving, and I will explore those in much more detail in the second book of this trilogy. For the time being, suffice it to say that forgiveness is where we find true healing and release. Then we can receive God's peace for the situation and move on.

In the Lord's prayer, we pray, "Forgive us the wrongs we have done as we ourselves release forgiveness to those who have wronged us" (Matthew 6:12, TPT). Even as the Roman soldiers were pounding nails through Jesus's wrists, "He prayed over and over, 'Father, forgive them, for they don't know what they're doing'" (Luke 23:34, TPT). In the power of the Spirit, may you also be able to pray the same over the situations that have caused you so much sorrow. Don't let the enemy continue to victimize you by holding on to unforgiveness. Again, we will explore this issue in much more detail later.

Selah.

The Last Step—Dealing with Shame by Leaning into Jesus

You are so close to walking out of the cave of false guilt and shame now. There's a light before you that is stunningly brilliant in its radiance. It is Jesus! He is telling you that there's one more thing he wants you to understand. He wants to give you another revelation of the cross, but you need a little background first to grasp it well.

In the days of ancient Rome, crucifixion was the most humiliating of deaths. It was meant to be that way, both to punish the criminal as well as to deter others who would consider disrupting the order of the Roman Empire. The felon would first be flogged, lashed up to forty times with a whip that had jagged pieces of lead and bone chips fastened to the ends of leather straps. It wasn't unusual for the whipping alone to kill a person.

The offender would then be forced to carry the crossbeam of the cross on his back while being paraded down "Main Street" to a hill just outside the city walls. Roman officials wanted to ensure that everyone in town could witness the degrading spectacle to maximize its effect. The victim would then be nailed to the cross and hoisted above the crowd.

Out of respect, painters and sculptors through the ages have depicted scenes of the crucifixion with a loincloth wrapped around Jesus's genitals, but that is not how crucifixion occurred. Roman soldiers stripped a person *naked* before nailing or tying him to a cross. The condemned outlaw would then hang in full public view, sometimes for days, as he writhed to breathe. Truly, the cost of defying Rome was steep.

At some point, exhaustion or dehydration would set in, and the fellow would die. If the process was dragging on for too long, the Roman soldiers would intervene by literally breaking the legs of the rebel so he could no longer push himself up to catch his breath.

So, let's blow out the sides of the box here. Adam, who represented humanity, *hid behind a tree* after he sinned. Jesus, the "last Adam," also represented humanity on the cross. Instead of hiding behind a tree, he received the hideousness of all sin, the load of all guilt, and the dishonor of all shame for the entire human race into his very own body and was *raised up on a tree* for all to see.

Adam used fig leaves to cover his guilt and shame. Jesus had no fig leaves to hide behind, nor did he want them. He allowed himself to be "exposed" so that the utter depravity, horror, and disgrace of the sin, guilt, and shame of the world were on full display symbolically in his physical nakedness. Second Corinthians 5:21 (TPT) puts all of this into the starkest of terms: "For God made the only one who did not know sin to become sin for us, so that we who did not know righteousness might become the righteousness of God through our union with him."

Are you catching this? The cross changes everything for the believer. It gives us right-standing before God! In his own great humiliation as our human representative, Jesus bore our sin, guilt, and shame so we would no longer have to bear it. He died so that that we could live in his freedom, and that applies to *every* area of our lives—guilt, false guilt, and shame included.

In him, we are totally acceptable to our Father-God ... forever! Here is a sampling of verses to help you grab on to the truths of these revelations:

> Now Christ lives his life in you! And even though your
> body may be dead because of the effects of sin, his

life-giving Spirit imparts life to you because you are fully accepted by God. (Romans 8:10, TPT)

Therefore, accept each other just as Christ has accepted you so that God will be given glory. (Romans 15:7, NLT)

As it is written: "See, I lay in Zion a stone that causes people to stumble and a rock that makes them fall, and the one who believes in him will never be put to shame." (Romans 9:33, NIV)

As Scripture says, "Anyone who believes in him will never be put to shame." (Romans 10:11, NIV)

As we meditate on and internalize these promises of the Bible into our identity in Christ on a regular basis, we push shame out the back door. We enter into an abiding sense of the presence of Christ within us. We can rest in the heart-knowledge of the truth that we have right-standing with God by faith in the finished work of Jesus on the cross. When God forgives us, he forgives us! Period! It's over. That's the absolute certainty we must believe to overcome guilt and shame.

If you want a wild example of how completely God can forgive, check 2 Timothy 1:3. The apostle Paul writes this letter to Timothy, his protégé, and starts it out with a comment about how he serves God with "a clear conscience."

A clear conscience? Seriously? This is *Paul*, the same guy who was passionately murdering Christians not many years before penning those very words! How could he possibly have a clear conscience? Because, through the cross, Paul was able to lay aside the weight of guilt and shame that could have ruined him and minimized his amazing ministry. He understood the power of the cross working in his life to set him free from his past! Hear his words: "But I focus on this one thing: forgetting the past and looking forward to what lies ahead, I press on to reach the end of the race and receive the heavenly prize for which God, through Christ Jesus, is calling us" (Philippians 3:13–14, NLT).

His Joy, Our Joy

This angle on Jesus taking our sin, guilt, and shame to the cross is intense. He predicted how he would die multiple times to his disciples in the three-plus years he had with them. During that time, I'm sure all kinds of ideas churned in Jesus's mind as he pondered his chosen mission for those he cherished so much.

Hebrews 12:1–2 (NASB) provides a tiny snippet, just one of Jesus's thoughts, as he looked ahead to the agony of the cross. I have little doubt that this reflection often captured Jesus's heart: "... and let's run with endurance the race set before us, looking only at Jesus, the originator and perfecter of the faith, who for the joy set before Him endured the cross, despising the shame, and has sat down at the right hand of the throne of God."

Did you catch that? Jesus despised the shame because of "the joy set before Him." We usually think that arriving in the place of honor beside God's throne was "the joy set before Him," and that interpretation totally fits the context of the verse. But personally, I don't believe that was foremost in Jesus's mind.

Jesus was so insanely in love with those who would choose to follow him that "the [true] joy set before Him" right before he went to the cross was ... *you*! And it was *me*! The thought of us being set free from the bondage of sin and all the guilt and shame that goes with it always captivated our Savior as he considered the torment that lay ahead. It was always his dream that authentic, open, loving communion with him could be restored forever. We are always "the pearl of great price" to him.

Take hold of this twist on that same verse as it applies to us. Because of the joy set before us and the joy who lives within us right now (Jesus!), we can also despise any shame the enemy hurls at us. "If God is for us, who can be against us?" (Romans 8:31, NIV).

No matter what should come our way on this earth, Jesus will always be with us. He will always love us. He will always accept us. We sing the song of our lives for the audience of One and it electrifies him. He is always our joy, and he is always more than enough.

Selah.

Prayer

Father-God,

I don't even know how to begin. Help me to forgive those who planted such horrible images about myself in my mind, and help me to forgive myself for believing those lies for so many years. I bind the spirits of false guilt and shame in my life. They no longer have a hold on me, in Jesus's name! From now on, I renounce false guilt, shame, and the grief that goes with them. I renounce any sense of unworthiness; I renounce the lie that I am a failure. I renounce the lie that I am not enough, and I renounce the false identity that I built for myself based on shame.

I replace those lies with the truth that I am complete in your Son, Christ Jesus. I am your special creation, fearfully and wonderfully made to bring you glory in and through my life. I thank you that you forgive and cleanse me of my sin, guilt, and shame—that you do not condemn me, that I am worthy of your love in Christ Jesus, and that you accept and cherish me as a child, just as I am, with all my faults.

Thank you that whom the Son sets free is free indeed (John 8:36). I declare freedom from guilt and shame! Thank you, Father, that I can rest secure in your love! You are the one who gives my life true value and significance. Reveal the truths and promises of Your Word to my heart so that I can lean into you more and grow into the image of your Son Jesus.

In the mighty name of Jesus, I pray. Amen.

Key Summary Points:

- Shame is rooted in lies. Satan is the father of lies.

- Satan's purpose is to steal, kill, and destroy, but Jesus came to give us life (John 10:10) and to destroy the works of the evil one (1 John 3:8).

- True guilt is a red flag that we have chosen sin in some area of our lives and need to address it.

- Repentance is changing our minds—turning from sin and turning to God, who has given us the victory over sin and its power.

- Conviction is from the Holy Spirit; condemnation is from the enemy.

- False guilt is guilt that has no true basis in fact or it can be the ongoing feeling of guilt even after we have confessed our sins to God and repented of them. False guilt is frequently rooted in difficulty in receiving God's forgiveness or in forgiving ourselves.

- Guilt and false guilt are about what we do, our behavior. Shame is about identity, who we perceive ourselves to be. Ultimately, what shame comes down to is a personal sense of unworthiness of the love and attention of others or of God.

- The cross changes everything for the believer. No longer do we have to hold on to shame for our failings or carry the shame others have put on us. In Christ Jesus, we are totally acceptable to our Father-God, *forever*. Jesus was disgraced and shamed so that we could live free from that guilt and shame.

- We do not need to succumb to the lies that we are not worthy of his love, not worthy to be forgiven, or not worthy of his amazing plans for our lives. In Christ, our spiritual DNA has been altered. Guilt and shame no longer have a right to have a hook in us. They are *not* who we are!

Reflection and Discussion Questions:

1. What is the difference between true guilt, false guilt, and shame?

2. Which of Satan's arrows of false guilt has been the most difficult for you to deal with? Why? What is the lie behind the arrow?

3. Think of a time when you felt shame. Describe how you felt inside. Do you think you would feel differently about that situation today? If so, why?

4. Do you agree with Dr. Brown, "that vulnerability is the core of shame and fear and our struggle for worthiness"? Why or why not?

5. Are you in a situation now where a person is laying a guilt/shame trip on you? How will you set a boundary with that person so that you don't need to receive his condemnation and shame any longer? Ask the Holy Spirit to guide your words and actions.

6. What one thing impacted you the most from this chapter? Why?

7. Did leaning into Jesus at the end of this chapter give you a better understanding of the shame he endured on the cross? How does that foster greater trust in God in your journey?

CHAPTER 2

Slaying the Demons Within:
Fear and the Orphan Spirit

Do not fear, for I have redeemed you; I have called you by name; you are Mine! (Isaiah 43:1, NASB1995)

But in the day that I'm afraid, I lay all my fears before you and trust in you with all my heart. What harm could a man bring to me? With God on my side, I will not be afraid of what comes. (Psalm 56:3–4, TPT)

There is no fear in love; but perfect love casts out fear, because fear involves punishment, and the one who fears is not perfected in love. (1 John 4:18, NASB1995)

And you did not receive the "spirit of slavery," leading you back into the fear of never being good enough. But you have received the "Spirit of full acceptance," enfolding you into the family of God. And you will never feel orphaned, for as he rises up within us, our spirits join him in saying the words of tender affection, "Beloved Father!" For the Holy Spirit makes God's fatherhood real to us as he whispers into our innermost being, "You are God's beloved child!" (Romans 8:15–16, TPT)

Ah! So good to see you have emerged from the cavern of false guilt and shame victoriously! Congratulations! Good for you. It was not easy, but you did it. You will find as we continue to explore the deep of these caves that you will gain momentum. You will become stronger and swifter of foot. You will wield your sword with greater ease.

Why? Because you have already started to shed the weight of these burdens. Just like Hebrews 12:1 (NLT) encourages us, "Strip off every weight that slows us down, especially the sin that so easily trips us up. And let us run with endurance the race God has set before us." False guilt and shame are gone. Fear and the orphan spirit will soon follow.

We press on to this chasm of fear. She has claimed many victims. Some have sought to hunt her down, only to get lost in the maze of tunnels that branch from her primary den—the side trails of anxiety, depression, insomnia, rage, and even indifference, among others. But we will not get lost this time with Jesus to guide us. Remember, he came to save … the lost. And he will not fail us now.

Our strategy? We will hide and wait for this dragon to come to us because fear seeks us out regularly. But it's not just any fear that we need to lay low. The one we await is the big mama of all fears: the fear of rejection or abandonment. She is the beast who gives birth to the brood of all other fears. But this time … *this* time, we will take her by surprise!

Once we have overcome her, we will set fire to this dingy lair so that it and its web of paths shall crumble once and for all—because Jesus came to set the captives free. Freedom is his gift to us. It *belongs* to us. The fear of rejection has stolen it from us, but it is ours … and in Christ Jesus, we shall have what is ours! This night, at long last, we will lie down to sleep in peace. The dragon mistress of this wicked den will fall because perfect love casts out all fear, and Perfect Love is with us. And he is in us. And he is for us.

Come! Let us go forth!

Roots of Fear

The Breadth of Fear—Jamal's Cavern

Jamal was a middle-aged man, tense, with sagging, dark bags under his eyes. And he was wired, I mean super wired, when he came to us.

"I am afraid of everything!" he announced loudly, a second after sitting down. "When I was a kid, I would curl up in a ball under my covers and keep a little hole open so I could still see things in the room. I remember, one time, stringing pots up in front of the kitchen door so that, if anyone tried to break in, I would hear them and could protect my family. Even now, I wake up after about three or four hours and am wide awake. I am always tired. I feel like a dirtball."

Jamal's "plate" was overflowing, and it was spilling all over the table as we tried to understand how to pray with him. His father was unavailable emotionally. With few exceptions, even when he would have some small victory as a child, Jamal's dad would lasso him in with, "Now, don't get a big head! Make sure you don't get a big head about this, Jamal!" There was minimal celebration of Jamal's positive accomplishments.

The story only went downhill from there. When he was just a young boy, his dad was shot and barely survived. Throughout his childhood, Jamal continued to be petrified that his father would die, but he didn't. A few years later, however, his dad's gambling led to the loss of their family home, another terrifying event.

As for his mother—well, "She did the best she could," Jamal defended her. His mama did believe in God, but somewhere along the way, her theology got twisted into an occult-laden approach to life. Everything got demonized. Anything bad that happened was "of Satan," or "that's from the occult." She literally planted and nurtured fear in his heart almost every day. Then, unlike his father, who almost passed away, Jamal's mother did die in a car accident when he was ten. From that day on, he was pretty much on his own. The little guy became a child fending for himself, trying to steer through the complexities of survival when he should have been out playing ball with his friends.

"Then there was my big sister. She teased me big time when I was a kid. She was *merciless*. I hated it. *I hated it!* In school, I would get into trouble because I beat up the bullies. I just couldn't take it!"

Several times, he blamed himself for his bad decisions. "I should've known better." At other times, he excused his parents with, "They did the best they could. I love them. They did the best they could."

Even at a young age, Jamal hurled through life unprotected and abandoned—physically and emotionally—with no substantive spiritual input to speak of. Was it any wonder that fear and anxiety plagued him day in and day out?

"I'm just tired of fighting. I'm tired of feeling like a dirtball," he said with a sigh.

As the Holy Spirit spoke to him, Jamal began to see how his fear and self-loathing were protective mechanisms. They kept him from facing his pain, from facing how his family had left him an emotional orphan, from facing the unwise choices he had made in his life, and from facing who he was—or who he thought he was: "a dirtball." He was willing to release the fear and to forgive those who had abused his heart. Over the course of the session, he came to understand that he was never truly alone; he was not an orphan. Jesus was always there and grieved over what was happening to him.

As we continued to pray, something shifted in Jamal. He began to see his identity as a beloved son of God. Accepted, cherished, and celebrated by a Father who loved him. By the time he left, his facial appearance and demeanor were noticeably transformed. He was more relaxed, peaceful.

"That's where God wants you to live, Jamal, all the time," I encouraged him.

There was a long way to go for complete healing, but Jamal had a great start.

When Fear First Crept In

The dragon of fear had so many tentacles wrapped around Jamal, he didn't know where to begin to get free. Perhaps you feel like that on some days. Or maybe you feel like fear leads you around all the time. Unfortunately, I saw the stranglehold of anxiety around the lives of children and young adults regularly in my medical practice.

Fear is a cruel taskmaster. But take note: all the tentacles of fear trying to smother Jamal—of people trying to break into his home, of not being able to get enough sleep, of demons hiding under every rock, of getting bullied at school, of his father dying, and whatever else—they were not the real problem. They were just the tentacles. You won't kill the dragon if you're only trying to slice off a limb. No, you need to thrust your sword into the heart of this demon; that's the only way she will fall.

So, where do we begin? What is the true core of fear? What is the root of all the anxiety, worry, rage, and other facets of fear I mentioned earlier? Again, let's go back to the original couple, Adam and Eve, for some clues. Recall that their first reaction after the Fall was shame, but the second was *fear*. "Then the Lord God called to the man, and said to him, 'Where are you?' [Adam] said, 'I heard the sound of you in the garden, and I was afraid because I was naked; so I hid myself'" (Genesis 3:9–10, NASB).

Here's the question—what were Adam and Eve afraid of, exactly? In

Genesis 3:10, Adam says he was afraid "because I was naked." How the Fall impacted sexuality is definitely a topic worthy of discussion, but this book is not the place for it, and this is not the time. Let's step back and try to understand the broader picture of what was happening here.

Think on Adam's words for a moment. "I heard the sound of you in the garden, and I was afraid because I was naked." If taken literally, Adam's words don't make a whole lot of sense. He and Eve were just as naked *before* the Fall as they were after, and it never bothered them then. So, why now? (See Genesis 2:25.)

No, the wider lens for us is to consider what Adam meant by *naked* more metaphorically—that he and his wife were uncovered, that the evil in their hearts had suddenly been exposed, as I mentioned in chapter 1. Maybe they feared that God would discover their failure and that it would displease him. Or that he would be horribly upset. Or perhaps they were afraid of this whole idea of death. Remember, God had told them they would "surely die" if they ate of the fruit.

Park there for just a moment. Prior to their disastrous choice, Adam and Eve had absolutely no idea what the term *death* meant because it was the garden of *Paradise*. There was no death in Paradise! There was no grid for them to comprehend death. The wolf could play with the lamb, the lion could lie down with the calf; all life forms could rest side by side in total harmony and peace. Something certainly changed in their bodies after the Fall, but Adam and Eve were still alive physically, hiding behind a tree, no less! No, not even physical death was their primary fear at that moment.

Let's pan back from the scene a little bit more. Adam and Eve first experienced shame after the Fall—that they were not good enough for God anymore, that they weren't worthy of his love. After he had trusted them with everything on earth that was worth having, they failed miserably! In combination with their shame, however, fear simmered up to the surface from the depths of their being, like two children who had just received all Fs on their report cards.

So, let me ask a question. What do you do when you first see all those giant, 40 font Fs etched in red on your laptop screen that you know your parents will see that evening? You hide their laptop. You bury it in the laundry, praying it will run through a cycle before they find it. You try to get it to crash. You tell your dog to dig up a nice, big hole for it in your neighbor's yard. You obviously can't let your parents see it because they would be horribly disappointed in you—so disappointed, in fact, that they might *reject* you.

If you were old enough, things could really deteriorate. Your parents might even say, "That's it! We're not putting up with this garbage anymore. We've had enough! You're eighteen now. These grades are totally unacceptable. We've given you *so* many chances, and you continue to blow it. You need to move out. Now! We don't want you around anymore!"[12] So, the unthinkable could occur. With your colossal failure, your parents might even *abandon* you. Now we've hit on something!

The deep-down fear that gripped this exquisite couple after the Fall was that their one true love, the One who had cherished them so dearly, would reject them or, worse yet, abandon them because—catch this now— *that's what true death is*: absolute, eternal separation from God. That's the essence of God's caution to them that "you shall surely die." That's why they felt so helpless. You can almost see them huddling together as they frantically tied the fig leaves around their waists. "How do you think God is going to deal with this? Do you think he'll know? He warned us, remember? 'You will surely die.'"

During the first panic attack on planet earth, the couple was experiencing the staggering weight of *spiritual* death firsthand, even before Jesus returned to the garden to look for them, and it was crushing them. Yes, there was a change in their physical bodies with the Fall. Yes, the Fall also impacted their souls in a hugely negative way—the peace that permeated their minds, wills, and emotions was definitely gone. But what troubled the two so immensely was that they sensed a major transformation in their innermost beings, their spirits. There was spiritual separation from their Creator now that didn't exist before. The thought that God could possibly *completely* forsake them was excruciating. In fact, it filled them with … *fear*. Unimaginable fear. There was no way they could bear to face this God who had been such an amazing, sweet, faithful, loving friend to them day by day.

What they did not know was that God had a backup plan. A substitute. An animal sacrifice—the shedding of animal blood to cover their sins, and the death of that animal instead of their own physical death, for the time being. It was all a temporary fix, to be sure, but it did restore a semblance of relationship with God. It would suffice until the time came for Jesus, the perfect sacrifice, to be offered for all humanity for all time.

We need to unwrap this more.

Selah.

Reflection:

Imagine that you were Adam or Eve. What do you think your first response would have been after you ate of the forbidden fruit and could sense a dramatic shift within you?

Fear of Rejection or Abandonment

When we mess up in our relationships with God through what we might consider some big failure, we usually become fearful of what God might do. We often have this picture of God as an angry, old grump just waiting for us to do something wrong so he can pull out his oversized, heavenly flyswatter and whack us a good one. That is such a distortion of who he truly is. But our own mistakes are only one reason we fear. At other times, concern about potential traumatic events completely out of our control can also trigger fear within us. Will God be there in that moment to protect us or a loved one? Will he provide for us in a time of need? Will he heal us when we are ill? How will things turn out?

When my family and I moved to the West Coast to attend seminary, the first few weeks just shattered us. One thing after another seemed to go wrong. *What was happening?* Jeanie and I were paralyzed with fear. After another unanticipated piece of bad news, Jeanie was beside herself. In a forlorn tone, she mumbled her thoughts aloud to me, "We must've done something horribly, horribly wrong." Of course, the unspoken phrase at the end of her sentence was, "for God to treat us like this."

Back then, we didn't really know the love of our Father-God like we do now. But our perception of what was happening to us is exactly how most believers view the bad things that come their way. "I must've done something really bad for this to be happening to me. Otherwise, God never would have allowed it." So, what is the root of all these fears, the big-time mama fear of all fears? Plain and simple: When you go to the heart of all the different fears we contend with in life, it all funnels down to the fear of rejection or abandonment in one way or another.

Look at Adam and Eve after they had sinned. They hid behind a tree and tried to cover up. For them, it was akin to saying, "I don't want to be seen. I don't want *to be known*. I am afraid to be known for who I am now because, if you really know who I am, you might reject me. You might even leave me." That's the root—we are afraid God will reject or abandon us, leaving us hopelessly alone in this world. Such a dreadful, depressing thought. But it's a thought that has crossed every one of our minds. That's what Jeanie and I were thinking in the midst of our California distress. "All this bad stuff must be happening because God is mad at us. He is rejecting us."

How about a current example of how various fears ultimately boil down to the fear of rejection or abandonment? As I am completing another draft of this book, the COVID-19 pandemic is striking the globe with astounding force. Let's imagine you are anxious about losing your job, or maybe you've already lost it. You are the only wage-earner in your family. If you allow fear to overcome you in this predicament, your thoughts might run something like this: "No job means I have no income. No income means I can't provide for my family adequately. That means we will need to cut back in significant ways to make sure we have food, a roof over our heads, and that we still have electricity. Not sure how long I can handle this because we don't have that much saved up." (A feeling of dread takes hold of you now.) This elicits a fear that God is not really looking after you, not really providing for and protecting you the way he's supposed to—otherwise, why would this be happening? That prompts a fear that God is not trustworthy. For some unknown reason, he has chosen not to help you in your time of need. You are on your own to deal with the crisis.

Now, you could focus on the individual fears here: no job, no income, no place to live, the inability to afford basic necessities, and so on. But really, the thing that revs up the hurricane in your stomach is the fear that you are on your own. Alone. With no one to help you—and you're just not so sure you can make it. What is the "translation" of the feeling that you are completely

74

on your own? It's that God has abandoned you. That you can't depend on him. That the promises in Scripture that claim he will take care of you are not true. Please understand, you may not consciously be thinking that, but that's really what you're saying when you convince yourself that you're on your own.

Do you see how Satan ramps up the fear whirlwind? Like I said, he's not that clever. He uses the exact same deception on us that he used in the garden of Eden. He instills doubt about God being worthy of our trust and about the truthfulness of His Word. The devil's mantra to us is that "God does not have your back."

What about Jamal's story? Fear of abandonment by God goes hand in hand with fear of abandonment by others in our lives. Jamal never shared whether or not he grew up in the hood, but he felt compelled to tie pots and pans to a rope across the kitchen door so that, if anyone tried to break in, he (as a little kid!) would wake up and could protect his family. Why? Because he didn't believe anyone else would protect them, not even his dad! The thought of something bad happening to his family, that's what scared him the most. (Unspoken meaning: "If something bad happens to my family, I will be alone, abandoned in this world.") The sad reality was that, even at such a tender young age, he was already on his own on many levels.

Jamal's situation as a young boy is a good example because the fear of rejection or abandonment takes shape very early in childhood. What happens when a young child loses sight of a parent in a grocery store, even for a moment? Total panic. Hysteria. Uncontrollable crying until the parent returns to comfort him or her. Or the child who comes up with endless excuses so the parent has to return to his or her room at bedtime: "I'm thirsty." "I have to go to the bathroom." "Can't you tell me just one more story?" We call it separation anxiety in pediatrics, but anxiety is just a more socially acceptable term for fear. Remember what Dr. Brené Brown said in chapter 1? "What we know is that connection, the ability to feel connected, is—neurobiologically, that's how we're wired." Every normal human being is "wired" for connection. Therefore, when connection is threatened, fear will arise.

Here's the thing—in the eyes of Father-God, believers are his children, children with the same basic needs of love, affirmation, provision, protection, security—no matter how old we are. Ongoing rejection and abandonment are the worst nightmares of any healthy person because they beckon the "grim reaper" of complete disconnection and loneliness. All those essential needs of a human being get called into question when you are disconnected because there is no one to provide them to you. So, when you get right down to it, loss of connection is really what the fear of rejection and abandonment are all about.

Childhood and the Scourge of Fatherlessness

I cannot begin to describe how powerful a force this issue of fear of rejection or abandonment is in our lives. Whether as a physician or a pastor, I have encountered a host of children and adults with broken hearts because they were either physically or emotionally abandoned by one or both parents when they were young. Here they were in my office, decades later, still grappling with the fallout of that abandonment. Oftentimes, they never truly got over it. Like shame, seeing life through a lens of rejection or past abandonment impacts *everything*.

The fatherlessness issue in our culture is particularly poignant in this regard. According to the US Census Bureau data of 2017, almost twenty million children, more than one in four, live without a father *physically* in the home. Talk about abandonment! These statistics I am laying out here should rattle you. Children growing up in a fatherless home:

- are almost four times more likely to be poor,
- are twice as likely to drop out of high school,
- are seven times more likely to become pregnant as a teen,
- are at a dramatically greater risk of drug and alcohol abuse,
- are more likely to commit a crime and go to jail, and

- have higher rates of behavioral and emotional health problems, including depression and suicide.[13]

Fathers are the ones who, by and large, impart identity to us and are supposed to be the ones who provide us with a safe environment to grow up in. That applies to both male and female children. I'm emphatically not saying that mothers aren't important in a child's upbringing, but there is no question that a tremendous, positive dynamic exists when a healthy dad is present in the home and is lovingly invested in his wife and kids.

Some may disagree with my claim that fathers impart identity to their daughters, but the Census Bureau summary of the consequences of fatherlessness is strongly compelling for *both* males and females. There is one organization, The Fatherless Daughters Network, which attempts to inspire women past fatherlessness. In their powerful web video, they assert that "the hallmark trait of a fatherless daughter [is] fear of loss or abandonment."[14]

Selah.

Reflections:

Think of a time when you were fearful in your younger years. What were you afraid of? Why? Ask the Holy Spirit to help you trace the fear backward. Does it bring you to a root fear of rejection or abandonment in some way?

Can you recall a time when you felt rejected or abandoned during your childhood? How did that make you feel? It likely robbed you of self-worth, right? Do you see how fear and shame are "siblings"? They often travel together, just as they did for Adam and Eve.

Where Does That Leave Us?

You may be wondering, "How does this relate to me? Why do we need to get into this rejection and abandonment stuff? Everything was fine with me and my family. Things were good growing up." It's possible that this section doesn't relate to you at all. But remember—we are in the cavern of fear, talking about those things that make it uncomfortable for us to truly trust God. Over 25 percent of homes in the United States don't have a father physically present, and that doesn't include fathers who aren't present emotionally. So, you can probably double that 25 percent, at the very least!

If you've grown up in a home where a parent (and especially your dad) rejected you or abandoned you physically or emotionally, it leaves a vacuum in your heart and soul, a father-wound. For many, life becomes a search for someone or something to fill the vacuum. Unfortunately, for those with a deep father-wound, the hole of earthly rejection or abandonment becomes the lens through which they view their heavenly Father. Trying to connect with God then becomes a long, challenging journey of learning to trust him. The reality is that he is the only One who can fill that void adequately, but the hesitation to trust him tends to hover in the back of our minds without us even being aware of it.

Though we're all made in "the image of God," the real question if you're one of the many with a father-wound is this: what is *your* image of God? How do you perceive who he is to you right now? Do you have a nagging fear that your heavenly Father will reject or leave you, just like your earthly father did? Perhaps you are like Adam and Eve—you hide. It may appear that finding solace in the dark of this cave of fear is a good fix, but deep down, you know that's not true.

Again, what is your image of God? Do you feel at ease talking to him about the things that matter to you in life? Maybe you don't even want to deal with it. It's just too painful. So understandable. The problem with that approach, of course, is that your relationship with God will always be one of distance—compromised, just as it was with your own father. That will make it extraordinarily difficult to come to a place of trusting him and finding peace in your life. Your relationship will always be marked by some degree of suspicion or doubt. That's precisely why we need to confront this dragon.

Selah.

The other thing I have found in so many young adults who hold to "this rejection stuff doesn't really apply to me" is that many live in serious denial about how "good" things actually were growing up in their families of origin. Because of this subconscious self-deception, they are unable to recognize or acknowledge the significant dysfunction in their families and how it has negatively impacted their lives.

Part of the reason for this denial is that we were taught to "honor our parents," and we absolutely *do* want to honor them. I mean, that's one of the Big Ten (Commandments), right? We will talk more about honoring our parents in book two of this trilogy, but let me simply say this for now: we honor our parents by respecting them with the love and grace of the Lord. We honor God by recognizing what is unhealthy from our childhoods and laying it at the foot of the cross where the blood of Jesus can wash it from us and heal us. We do not need to hold on to any toxic behaviors that were modeled for us or to absorb any damaging words that were spoken into our lives. Exploring truth with the Holy Spirit does not dishonor parents.

Please take the time to unwrap this monumental issue with the Holy Spirit. If we do not discern and deal with family dysfunction, it will not go away on its own. In fact, if we don't process "the baggage" from the past, we are destined to repeat the same ungodly behaviors in our own lives and re-create them in our own children. Why? Because of Galatians 6:7 and many other similar verses: "For whatever a person sows, this he will also reap" (NASB). In other words, what has been "sown" into us as children will reap a harvest in our lives, for better or for worse. If we don't intentionally pull out the roots of any "weeds" that our parents sowed into us, those same weeds will be reproduced in us and through us to our own children! When God said that each would reproduce after its own kind in the book of Genesis, he wasn't only talking about biology!

Here's what I mean. I attended to the medical needs of many college students in my pediatric practice. (Once they finished college, I would move them on to an "adult" doctor.) Over the years, I had some of them tell me they had no relationships of value with their fathers (much more common than a "mother-wound").

"How are you doing with that?" I would ask.

"It's okay. I'm fine with it," they would assert with a shrug of the shoulders.

I didn't buy that line for a minute. Without inner healing, it was only a matter of time before the voids in their hearts would suck them in to some self-destructive mode, outwardly or inwardly, as a coping mechanism. Alcohol was a common go-to. More often than not, their dads had the exact same alcohol problem. Let's follow how this pattern evolves.

What happens in the minds of children and adults when they have repeatedly been rejected or abandoned by a parent is very predictable. To believe that the person who fathered you or the mother who gave birth to you considers you of such little worth that he or she doesn't even want to associate with you is total devastation. Tremendous shame sets in. That shame triggers self-loathing. When the self-loathing gets bad enough, it works into depression, anxiety, and anger. Those who have been rejected or abandoned are angry at the parent(s) for not being there for them, for sure, but they are also angry at themselves because they feel there must be something wrong with them to have caused the parent(s) to leave.

As the anger gets externalized, it shows up in all kinds of ways: violence, road rage, an aggressive personality, gang membership, and so on. Other coping mechanisms besides alcohol include substance abuse, porn, a work addiction, acting out sexually, partying, busy-ness, the list goes on. Even excessive video-gaming is now recognized as an addiction. Again, these individuals are *frequently* in denial. They are simply not in touch with this root of rejection as the primary reason why they behave in such destructive ways nor do they perceive how harmful their behaviors are!

Of course, all these choices are escapes. They may make you feel good temporarily, but afterward, they leave you worse off than you were beforehand. More guilt. More shame, and no change in your anxiety level. Yet so many persist in going down these roads because they believe it is easier than processing the emotional shrapnel from the rejection of a parent or from the belief that God is abandoning them. The enemy plants this self-defeating idea in our minds that numbing the rejection is better than bringing it to God for healing. "If I can't feel it, then it can't hurt me," is the underlying deception.

Only when we grab hold of the truth that the pain of staying in denial is much, much worse than the pain of going through the process of healing—only then can we begin to work toward wholeness in Christ.

Selah.

Reflections:

Being totally honest now—growing up, what was your relationship like with your parents? What about now, if they are still alive? How has your relationship with your parents impacted your life for better, worse, or both?

Take time before you answer these questions. A good gauge of your relationship with your parents is to ask yourself the question, "How comfortable was I going to Dad (or Mom) when I needed to talk to someone about something that was really important to me?"

Please hold on to these thoughts. We will try to work through them later in this chapter and in book two of the Deeper Trilogy. In the meantime, give thanks to the Lord for all the good your parents poured into your life.

The Orphan Spirit

The fear of rejection or abandonment is *always* accompanied to some degree by the "orphan spirit," the sense that you are on your own to face life because of how past hurts have affected you.[15]

As a pediatrician, I had plenty of contact with families who adopted children from foreign countries. Adoptive parents are close to the top of those on my heroes list. They are men and women of great courage, compassion, and faith, who are willing to take the life-long risk of welcoming children who are in need of care into their homes. Out of a heart of love they just want to make the world a better place for a child.

It wasn't unusual, however, for parents to share the frustrations they would occasionally experience in raising their adoptive children. Though there were often several factors that figured into their challenges, the main one was that the child(ren) never truly shed the orphan spirit. These youngsters had become "legal" sons and daughters, treated the same way as their biological kids—with the same blessings, same discipline, and same love. But some of the adoptees just had so much trouble shaking off their orphan identities. They never seemed to be able to rest securely in the love of their adoptive parents or to bask in their identities as "true" children. They remained orphans in spirit, unable or unwilling to connect in deeper, meaningful ways with others. They operated in a constant survival mode, navigating life under a cloak of suspicion and distrust rather than living life with confidence and in peace. It was awful to watch.

When you've never really experienced true love before, you doubt that it's real when it finally comes along. It doesn't fit the paradigm you developed in your mind as an "orphan"; unconditional love just can't find a place on your grid of life. So, what I saw in many of these children was an incessant restlessness gnawing deep in their souls. The uneasiness of that orphan spirit would manifest with the harmful behaviors I mentioned earlier, as you might imagine—acting out, relational problems, and so on.

Unfortunately, that same situation applies to many believers in our relationships to Father-God. "Legally," we understand that we become the adoptive children of God through Christ when we are born again. But we struggle spiritually to enjoy the freedom of feeling totally accepted by and acceptable to our Father-God. Because many of us didn't grow up with unconditional love, we're not sure what that looks like or, worse yet, if it's even real. We live in the same "home" with our Father-God-Dad, so to speak, but we don't connect with him in the ways he designed us to. If you want to read a compelling New Testament story that is a perfect illustration of this scenario, check out the story of the prodigal son and his older brother in Luke 15.

Where does that orphan spirit within us come from? We don't often think in these terms but, before his own fall, Satan was called Lucifer, "the angel of light"—a shimmering, brilliant, astoundingly magnificent creature in every way. Now, grab hold of this—God had created him. God was his (spiritual) *Father!* But Lucifer became proud. He believed the lie that he could be like God Most High.[16] In fact, he believed that he could actually supplant God. Needless to say, his plot failed.[17]

The first orphan to exist, then, was none other than Lucifer himself, the angel of light who evolved into the angel of dark. He intentionally separated himself from the love and protection of God to establish his own identity apart from his Maker. In so doing, this mighty angel lost his Father and his true identity. He became the prototype for all orphan spirits. He may not have become like God but, even to this day, he still pretends he has.

So, what does Lucifer do to imitate what God has already done? He tries to make humanity into *his* image, which is to say, into an orphan—alone, eternally separated from God. One of the most noxious effects of the Fall on humankind was that, in the moment that Adam and Eve ate of the forbidden fruit, the adversary unleashed an orphan spirit on them and therefore on all humankind. We must all confront the dragon of the orphan spirit at some point if we want to walk in the freedom of Christ.

We know the devil as the one who comes "to steal, kill, and destroy" us. Part of what he wants to steal from us is the heart-knowledge that we are beloved children of God. When he succeeds in that effort, he effectively molds us into his identity as an orphan. Here are some of the "orphan lies" he uses to isolate us from God:

> ➤ "You are alone, on your own. You'll just have to figure it out by yourself."
> ➤ "You are such a fool! God doesn't really care about you. Why would he? Look at who you are!"
> ➤ "There's no one to protect you now—you will just have to fight it out any way you can. That's what big boys and big girls have to do, you know. No more holding on to Daddy's hand."
> ➤ "God is not the provider he says he is. I mean, look at your situation right now! You will just have to keep slugging it out. So, don't ever have any expectation of getting ahead financially. It's always going to be hand-to-mouth for you and your family."
> ➤ "There's always going to be something. Sickness, family fighting, work problems. That's just the way life is, you know."

The orphan spirit tries to trap you in a "there's-no-way-out" mindset. Here's where the anger that accompanies the orphan spirit comes out. It becomes a coping mechanism of survival against the ongoing sense of hopelessness. I believe it's this anger that is behind much of the rising tide of inane acts of violence and lawlessness that characterize our world.

The orphan identity is what breeds the hatred behind the Hitlers and bin Ladens of this world, terrorist organizations, gangs, and the like.

Why would people ever want to join such groups? Because these groups, as dysfunctional and vicious as they are, provide an imitation family. Orphaned souls need somewhere to belong, *anywhere*! Like magnets, they attract each other because they need "family," even if the "family" is really sick! Remember Dr. Brown's assertion, "We were made for connection." For these lonely, orphaned souls, a pathological family connection is better than no connection at all. Their line of reasoning is, "At least I'm accepted here."

I have had to deal with an orphan spirit in my own life. I loved my father. He was a great dad in many respects, and I am truly grateful for the many positive things he modeled for me. And, unlike the way it is for many children, at least he was present in our home! But it was just not in him to call me up into godly manhood. Though he was a good provider and worked hard to create some wonderful opportunities for me, he was not there for me emotionally. He didn't know how to connect on a soul level. It was no coincidence that his own father was literally an orphan as a child. He was only following the pattern of what had been modeled for him by his own dad.

It took me a long time to grasp and accept the fact that my dad couldn't really give me what he didn't have himself. Parents who are weighed down by an orphan spirit will give rise to children with an orphan spirit. *We beget who we are*, on multiple levels. But we need to acknowledge and respect that our parents are doing the best they can do, and simply love them where they are at. We cannot expect more from them. But, as a young boy, I felt like I was on my own much of the time. That's when the "just not enough" mindset developed.

The kudos for me came from academic performance; I always did well in school (except for one term when I flunked Christian Doctrine!). Even the academic accolades rang hollow, though, because you will never really "arrive" if you derive your significance from anything apart from your identity in Christ. It's like the Superbowl MVP quarterback who is talking about "next year" just a few days after hoisting the Superbowl trophy high in front of a global audience! If my identity and value were rooted in my performance, how well I did in school or eventually from my profession as a physician—well, it just didn't satisfy the deep need of the soul. The tributes always fell short.

In retrospect, I came to understand that, even as a boy, I was on a mission to be fathered. I looked to teachers, professors, and even pastors to fill the gap. Though they were supportive and encouraging, most of them still had too much baggage of their own. They could not truly father me spiritually, either! That was a real bummer of a conclusion, but the truth was the truth. It was all so disheartening. After several decades of disappointment trying to find a desirable mentor, I came to see that I could only be fathered by God himself. He was the only One who could wash the orphan spirit away from who I was. Through much prayer, time in his presence, time in the Bible, counseling, and several resource books, I found my identity in Christ as a beloved son of God and could shed the orphan spirit. God is proud to be my dad, my *abba*—always. He is always looking for ways to help me do well and to conform me to the image of his Son. I continue to press into it.

Now, I am not saying that you shouldn't seek out good mentors, men and women who can shepherd you into godly manhood or womanhood. You absolutely should! But just be aware that leaders and mentors are not perfect—they cannot take you past where they are themselves. That includes parents, teachers, coaches, supervisors, and yes, even pastors sometimes. Just because these figures are in positions of authority in your life does not necessarily mean that they are whole! As I shared earlier, if you don't deal with your stuff, it doesn't go away, no matter who you are! But you can grant these people grace for where they are lacking, love them, and still learn much from them. The reality is that we are all in process during the journey.

Selah.

Reflections:

Are you plagued by a there's-no-way-out mindset—that you just have to do life on your own most of the time? What is the lie you are believing that is keeping you there? When did it start? How will you fight your way through it to get to the place of trusting God?

Suggestion: find a verse in Scripture that counters the lie and ask God to show you how to walk into that truth. For example, you might believe that you will always be playing catch-up financially, that "there's no way out." Philippians 4:19 (NASB) declares that "God will supply all your needs according to His riches in glory in Christ Jesus." As you pray about it, maybe the Lord will lead you to start taking night or weekend classes to transition into a different profession that will pay more. Or perhaps he will connect you with someone who can teach you how to steward your finances better. Allow the Holy Spirit to help you take an open-minded, creative approach to your circumstances.

Recognizing the Orphan Spirit

The orphan spirit runs rampant in our world. Whether in medicine, as a pastor, or simply in life, I regularly encounter people saddled with an orphan spirit. When you can acknowledge it in yourself and call it for what it is, it's much easier to see it in others.

The question, then, is this: how do you know if an orphan spirit is holding you back in your journey with the Lord? I will list some *possible* features of an orphan spirit as an aid. Let me underscore that this list is not exhaustive and is certainly not meant to belittle anyone because we all share at least a few of these traits.

My goal in putting this list together is twofold: first, to help you examine yourself for possible areas where you need God's healing touch; second, to serve as a guide for you as you seek out mature believers to mentor you. If you really want to grow, find people you know who are more mature in the Lord than you and connect with them. How do you identify these people? By the spiritual fruit you see in their lives. There is a caveat here, though. If you are serious about moving forward in God, you will need to risk being vulnerable, as we discussed in chapter one. Someone who knows Jesus well, however, will not violate your heart. He or she will guard it.

Consider these, then, as *possible* traits of those with an orphan spirit. It's not hard to see that there is a lot of overlap among these several categories:

Relational Difficulties:

- Those with an orphan spirit carry a spirit of rejection and abandonment. This is the hallmark. You can sometimes see it in their faces. Feeling like an orphan impacts life. Negativity and pessimism are common.
- They may be introverts, overly shy, or loners who hold back in relationships. They are afraid to join discussions or are reluctant to meet new people. On the other hand, they may be loud and overbearing—incessant talkers without a clue that they are rarely allowing others to speak. Their "conversations" are more of a monologue than a dialogue.
- They tend to believe people are out to get them or exploit them in some way. In other words, they may have significant trust issues from past wounds.
- Because they have difficulty trusting others and forming significant relationships, they often feel lonely, alienated, and disenfranchised. They may "know" a lot of people, but usually have few or no true friends they really feel close to.
- Orphans crave intimacy but have difficulty finding it. To compensate, they may create false intimacy with family members or friends. They do this by identifying a scapegoat within the family system (or circle of friends) so that "a common cause" exists for them to focus on with others in the system.
- They tend to form codependent relationships. Being a perpetual savior or enabler is not unusual because that approach keeps others dependent on them and makes them feel like they have value and purpose in life. On the other hand, they may be big-time people-pleasers who will do anything to avoid conflict or rejection.
- They may have difficulty submitting to authority or being held accountable, again because of trust issues.

- Orphans may become defensive when you try to correct them because they do not want to be perceived as being imperfect or weak. In their twisted way of thinking, imperfection or weakness will just elicit more rejection. Therefore, being vulnerable with others becomes difficult as well.

Insecurity:

- Orphan spirits are insecure and often critical of others in order to make themselves feel better about themselves. Sarcasm gets worked into what they say. The flip side of this is that orphans have difficulty celebrating others for who they are or what they've done. Insecurity is thus another major hallmark.
- They lack a strong sense of identity, but they still desire acceptance. So, they have difficulty saying "no" and setting appropriate boundaries with others. They sometimes allow people to take advantage of them unknowingly.
- Orphans not only have trouble setting boundaries with others, they also have trouble placing boundaries on themselves. Self-discipline can therefore be problematic. They may willingly compromise themselves to feel accepted and loved, even to the point of compromising themselves sexually. Of course, this love is not a godly love. It may temporarily soothe the pain of feeling alone in the world, but it invites more guilt, shame, and an even greater sense of isolation from God.
- Orphans may be hyper-religious, always helping out at church. They love having rules or requests to follow because they can succeed in those areas and get pats on the back at the same time. Unfortunately, over an extended period, they may overdo it and eventually become bitter, resentful, and burned out—especially if they are not getting recognized frequently.

- They can either be super controlling or overly reserved/self-effacing. Control may come out as anger or manipulation of others to get their way.
- They lack confidence and have a constant need for reassurance, another key feature.

Self-Focus:

- Those with an orphan spirit can be emotionally disconnected and are unknowingly "adult children." Because of their childlike, self-orientation, their agendas are more important to them than other people. When they are with you, conversations usually circle back to themselves—what they want to talk about, their opinions, or their needs.
- They can also be emotionally "over-connected." They fall in love out of a need to be needed, not understanding that this is another type of self-love rather than a mature love. Unfortunately, orphans tend to attract other orphans in relationships, again out of their neediness. This is a bad setup should the relationship progress towards marriage.
- Other people are there to serve the needs of the orphan, not to be empowered in the relationship, similar to how a child might act. This attitude sometimes leads to being socially inappropriate (e.g., being unusually demanding or not having a grateful attitude when it's fitting to do so).
- Another possible tip is that orphans frequently post relatively insignificant things about themselves on social media that most people don't really care about. They are looking for the attention and affirmation of others to prove to themselves that they do have value.

- A spin-off of their self-orientation is that they often play the role of the victim as a way of seeking sympathy and attention. They create unnecessary drama to keep the focus on themselves.

- Their realities are not true reality. They interpret life events differently than healthy people—namely, with themselves at the center of the world. They may have a false sense of self-importance or a distorted sense of what they are called to do. In a way, they can operate out of a kind of delusional spirit.

- No matter how good they try to make things look on the outside, orphans have low self-esteem and often loathe themselves. This is yet another key characteristic.

Performance Orientation (Very Much Linked to Insecurity):

- Successful performance is a means for orphans to "prove" self-worth—to themselves, to others, and to God. People with excessive perfectionistic tendencies or who are overly "hard drivers" almost always have some degree of an orphan heart.

- An unhealthy performance orientation may manifest in an addictive pursuit of wealth, possessions, power, influence, and so on. They look to these goals for significance.

- Appearances hold a lot of weight for them. They constantly ask, "How will this look to others?" They don't want to jeopardize the acceptance of or risk the rejection of others.

- Those with an orphan spirit may place an overemphasis on how they look physically—a preoccupation with weight, physique, and physical features. Sometimes, being a super-athlete becomes a way of proving oneself to others and even to him- or herself.

- Additionally, because they are themselves deceived, they may lie to appear confident and competent. In their lying, they are attempting to conform appearances to align with their realities. What is confusing to those who care about the orphan is that the person's lying is not done consciously; the person is unaware that he or she is twisting the truth or lying outright! The orphan sincerely believes that what he or she is telling you is factual.

Based on my professional experience, those with an orphan spirit are at higher risk for substance abuse and the psychosocial problems I alluded to earlier (e.g., anxiety, depression, rage) as well.[18]

Selah.

Reflections:

If you see yourself in some of the orphan descriptions above, take a deep breath and relax! *You are totally normal!* If you see yourself in a lot of them, you are struggling with an orphan spirit. Go through these various depictions again. As you do so, place a check mark next to the traits you feel are usually true of you.

Now, pick the one area that you feel is the toughest for you: relational difficulties, insecurity, self-focus, or performance orientation. Pray right now. Ask the Holy Spirit to reveal to you when you first noticed that area was difficult for you. What was going on in your life at that time that might have opened the door for the enemy to plant a lie in your heart about yourself? What was the lie?

Jesus Feels Our Pain

Several years ago, a young boy came into my medical office with his mother for his yearly physical exam. Per my norm, I asked him how he was doing, what fun things had been happening in his life, and what good things were coming down the pike. He told me he had just had his birthday the previous week, so of course I went ballistic over that—telling him how much he had grown, how strong he had become, and what a special day that must have been for him.

Throughout the visit, his demeanor seemed more subdued than I would have expected. When he needed to take a bathroom break, his mom filled me in on the real deal. "We threw a birthday party for him and invited about ten kids from his class," she began. "No one showed up." My heart sank. I tried to imagine the anguish this little guy must have experienced. It was obvious that he was still overwhelmed with the torment of it.

The spirit of rejection has been an ongoing global pandemic since the Fall. Everyone is afflicted to one degree or another. The major rejections can be difficult to overcome: divorce, a serious break-up, getting fired from a job, getting turned down by your backup school, and so much more. For those of you who are still processing rejection and its consequences, especially if you feel God has rejected you, we are going to take a brief but significant side-trail in this cavern of fear and the orphan spirit to help guide us back towards the light.

Jesus—the Orphan, Rejection, and Abandonment

It is beyond my imagination that the God of the universe would send his Son to become flesh and blood, to become "Emmanuel, God with us." Jesus understands us in every way because he was just like us. He faced plenty of rejection and abandonment during his lifetime on this earth and even knows what it's like to be an orphan. Let's dig in.

Jesus recognized the plight of orphans and widows in his culture and day well. He knew these individuals were among the most defenseless in the community. Without family to direct and protect them, they were weak, powerless, sometimes without rights, and vulnerable to the unscrupulous who would take advantage of them. In a real sense, widows and orphans were among "the abandoned of society," facing the harsh realities of life alone.

Now I cannot prove this, but I would like to put it out there for you to consider: Jesus may well have known firsthand what it was like to be an orphan. I say that because Hebrews 4:14 speaks of Jesus being able to sympathize with us in all our human frailties.[19] What most scholars presume is that Joseph, Jesus's earthly father, died sometime between the presentation of Jesus in the Temple at age twelve and the start of his ministry at age thirty. My personal belief is that Jesus was in his teens when Joseph passed away.

If that was indeed the case, it had to be a crushing season for Jesus. It meant the loss not only of his earthly father but of his mentor and dear friend. How many days they must've spent together in the heat of their carpentry shop as Joseph taught him how to work the wood into a creative masterpiece. In fact, the passing of Joseph could well have been the first time that Jesus confronted the earthly agony of death and the gut-wrenching sorrow of being separated from someone he loved so much. That part would be true for Jesus no matter how old he was when Joseph died. At the very least, Jesus could certainly grasp what life was like for a widow because he saw that in real time with his own mom, Mary.

For those of you who were abandoned by your father or mother, either physically or emotionally, know that Jesus understands your suffering. He sees your scars. He grieves your loss. And he weeps over how it has torn you apart. He has not forgotten you; he never will.

Some seven hundred years before Jesus was born, Isaiah says this prophetically of him: "Surely He has borne our griefs and carried our sorrows ..." (Isaiah 53:4, NKJV). So powerful. Jesus carried *your* griefs and *your* sorrows. You were never meant to carry the grief and sorrow of an orphan spirit long-term.

Selah.

So, there was a good chance Jesus knew what it was like to be a true orphan. And what about rejection and Jesus? Oh, wow! Jesus experienced rejection from just about every direction when he submitted to the will of his Father, and he still came out victorious ... and so can we! Let's go through this systematically because Jesus had to be one of the most rejected people who ever lived.

If you read through chapter 3 of the Gospel of Mark, you'll find Jesus teaching in a home after he had performed many miracles. The religious leaders are so distraught at the size of the crowds that are following Jesus that they try to persuade the people that the Prophet was casting out demons by the power of Satan! While this is going on, Jesus's family shows up outside the home. His *whole* family. His mother and *all* his brothers and sisters. That sounds a little over the top, but that's what it says.

Do you know why everyone in Jesus's family was tracking him down? They intended to take custody of him because—catch this now—they were saying, "He's out of his mind!" I'm not making this up! Check Mark 3:21 (NLT). That is the translation of the verse! His entire family had concluded that Jesus was insane.

Now, the real kick in the gut here for Jesus is that *his own mother* was with them too! Mary, the very woman who had become pregnant by the

Holy Spirit with Jesus! The one who had received multiple prophecies herself and from others about how extraordinary the child she had borne would be— "the Son of God Most High" who would reign over his people forever, so that "His kingdom will have no end."[20] Mary was right there with the rest of the clan! They *all* thought Jesus had lost it and planned to drag him home until he came to his senses.

Unfortunately, the rejection didn't stop there. Not *one* of his half-brothers or half-sisters was around when Jesus was tried, tortured, or executed on the cross. It was like you're on death row. The time of execution finally arrives, and not a soul from your family bothers to show up. Not one. (Sometime after the "he's insane" incident, however, Jesus's mother did have a change of heart because Mary was present during the crucifixion. But to be rejected by virtually his entire family had to be a tough hit for Jesus.) This picture of Jesus's rejection and abandonment is getting ugly, but we've still got more to get through.

In addition to his family, others even from within the ranks of his followers also concluded Jesus was not in his right mind and deserted him as well. *Lots of them.* Check out John 6. Jesus's words are just a little too far out there for them, so they walk. And what about Palm Sunday? The *masses* are shouting praises to Jesus as they wave their palm branches, saying, "Hosanna! Blessed is He who comes in the name of the Lord!" (John 12:12, NKJV). Only a few days later, the religious authorities instigate these same hordes to clamor for Jesus to be crucified! The civil authorities go along with the whole sham in order avoid a riot, which would have looked bad for them politically. So, they all leave Jesus to fend for himself. "If he's really the Son of God, let him come down from that cross and prove it!" they say to one another. (See Mark 15:32; my paraphrase.)

Finally, there were his closest friends, the twelve disciples. Jesus had poured himself into them for three and a half years—ate bread with them, taught them, trained them, and loved them. They had witnessed Jesus perform countless miracles to show them the heart of God. But Jesus knew what the Old Testament prophecies had predicted about him. "Strike the Shepherd and the sheep will be scattered" (Zechariah 13:7, NASB). Even Peter, one of the three disciples closest to Jesus, betrayed him to save his own neck.

Here is how Isaiah 53:3 (TPT) describes all these events: "[The Messiah] was despised and rejected by men ... We hid our faces from him in disgust and considered him a nobody, not worthy of respect." Oh, yes. Jesus understands rejection, abandonment, and betrayal quite well.

Let me encourage you. You don't have to carry rejection any longer. You don't have to allow an orphan spirit to shape you. You don't have to let a past abandonment define you. The key? Forgiveness. Forgiveness is always the key. I don't know your particular circumstances or the cruel ways you were scorned. Maybe it was the heartbreak of watching your father walk out the front door forever. Perhaps you were given a pink slip for someone else's mistake. Or your husband decided he just didn't love you anymore. I don't know. But the stinging, scarring memories linger. The cloud continues to drape your heart.

What I do know is that Jesus came to bind up your wounds and to heal your heart so you could move forward in your relationship with him and with others. I understand forgiveness can be difficult. It may seem totally impossible to you right now, but we have a God of the impossible! We will work through the challenges of forgiveness in book two of the Deeper Trilogy. Until then, please write down those areas you would like to explore more with the Holy Spirit.

Key Verses:

> Jesus said to them, "Haven't you ever read the Scripture that says: The very stone the builders rejected as flawed has now become the most important capstone of the arch. This was the Lord's plan—isn't it a miracle for our eyes to behold?" (Matthew 21:42, TPT)

However, those the Father has given me will come to me, and I will never reject them. (John 6:37, NLT)

No, I will not abandon you as orphans—I will come to you. (John 14:18, NLT) [This is Jesus's promise that he would send the Holy Spirit to be with the disciples after his crucifixion.]

Selah.

Reflections:

You now have a greater understanding of Jesus as an orphan, how he was rejected, and how he was abandoned by those he loved. We sometimes have a distorted view of who God is and blame *him* for the bad things that happen to us in life—including the rejection and abandonment we have experienced.

In the fullness of his humanity, do you now believe Jesus can identify with whatever rejection or abandonment you may have encountered? If not, what do you think the block is? If you do feel he can identify with you, how does that impact your trust level in God?

How to Slay This Dragon to Find Healing

What a great comfort to realize that Jesus understands the loneliness of being an orphan and the deep heartache of rejection and abandonment. It's like working at a company where you have a CEO who started on the lowest rung and works her way up to the top over the years. She knows exactly what it's like for you and every other person in the organization. She can understand your concerns, validate your feelings, and make necessary changes to company policy because she can identify with you every step of the way.

Jesus is our heavenly CEO. He experienced what we feel, firsthand. He suffered as we suffer, firsthand. He was tempted as we are tempted, firsthand. And he overcame, yet without sin. That is so beyond amazing. With his strength working in us, we must take the next step to engage the lies of the dragon of fear and rejection ourselves so that we too can overcome. Jesus has already defeated her. It is a finished work, but we need to lay hold of the spoils of freedom—to be rid of the rejection and to break free of the orphan spirit. How do we do that?

This may sound uncomfortably simple. I definitely am not trying to insult your intelligence and I know this will sound like a cliché, but there is only one way for you to slay this demon-dragon. You have to have an abiding revelation of God's love for you personally in the very, very deep of your heart and soul.

First John 4:16 (NASB1995) says this: "We have come *to know* and *have believed* the love which God has for us. God is love, and the one who abides in love abides in God, and God abides in him" (emphasis mine). Most Christians *know* God loves them, but it's a mind thing. It hasn't really seeped down to the heart. The heart is where the *believed* part of the verse comes in. It's when we get to the place of so believing that God loves us that we become totally secure in who we are in Christ … then the doors of the spirit realm swing wide open to us. We walk into the world of "all things are possible" with God rather than living a life constrained by our own efforts and built in our own strength.

A young woman recently shared that she has prayed for others with the heavy anointing of God on her and seen results. As an example, not long ago, she prayed for and witnessed a friend's healing. Yet, in the same conversation she confided that, although she knew God loved her friend, she still labored to believe that God loved *her*, delighted in *her*, and was head over heels about *her* on a personal level. That encapsulates exactly what I'm talking about and is so typical of Christians who love and serve the Lord faithfully. We know we love *him*, but we need to grasp how much he loves *us* much better than we do!

When you truly see and believe God for who he is and lay hold of what the cross means, you can internalize how much he is all about loving you. Then, do you know what happens? There's no room for fear. There's no room for the agony of rejection or abandonment. The orphan spirit is evicted because you have finally entered the place of rest and trust in Christ. Why? The words in 1 John 4:18 (NASB1995) say it all. Because "perfect love casts out fear."

Are you catching this? When you have the absolute, total assurance as a believer that Perfect Love, Jesus, dwells in you and loves you 110 percent, there is no room left for fear to take up space in your heart. It is cast out by default! The New Testament Greek word for "casts out" in this verse is a strong, forceful word, even violent!

This sounds a little paradoxical, but think of it this way. When you are truly "abiding" in the love of the Father like 1 John 4:16 says, this is what happens when fear tries to enter in. The Jesus-warrior in you rises up with the same fury Jesus had when he threw the money-changers out of the Temple. You proclaim with all boldness, "No! Get out, Fear! You don't belong here! There's no room for you here! Now get out!" The fragrance of the perfect love of Jesus completely permeating the room of your heart literally leaves not even one cubic millimeter of air space for the stench of fear to reside.

Ah, but you still struggle to believe this love that God has for you. It's too incredible. It's too far-fetched. It's just too simple, right? The stuff that a child's fairy tale is made of, but not real for the life you live in the twenty-first century.

So, how much does Jesus love you? Jesus left his heavenly throne to come to this earth to ransom *you* from the devil and from eternal death. He went to the cross *for you*. He paid the dearest of prices for *you*. He rose from the grave for *you*, so that his resurrection power to overcome fear could dwell *in you*. And he did all this while you were still a sinner, not because you were so wonderfully good! (See Romans 5:6–8.)

Even if you were the only one on the face of the earth, he still would have done it because you are worth that much to him. You are worth *that much*. Do you believe that? Do you really believe you mean that much to him? Getting over this stumbling block is a *huge* victory in learning to trust the Lord. Hear me on this, now. This sentence is one you should etch in your brain. *The value of something is determined by how much someone is willing to pay for it.* Please roll that around in your mind for a few minutes. The value of something is determined by how much someone is willing to pay for it.

God paid the ultimate price to "buy you back," to ransom you from the enemy. That's what a ransom is, right? A *massive* payout. It cost him big time, the life of his very own Son. That's how valuable you are to him. That's where your value comes from, Jesus. Only Jesus. He's all you need. He is enough. Your part is to rest in the beauty and grace of his love.

There's nothing more that God could possibly have done to demonstrate his love for you.

Here's another take on his love. Jesus called his Father *Abba*. That is an Aramaic word (the language the Jews spoke back then) that means, "dad," "daddy," "papa," or whatever affectionate term you might have for a father who loves you through and through. Even today, you can hear a child in Israel calling her dad *"Abba."*

I cannot begin to tell you how scandalously radical it was for Jesus to teach his followers to address the Creator of the universe as *Abba*. There is tenderness in *Abba*. Intimacy. Familiarity. Vulnerability. Trust. Faithfulness. Security. Protection. Provision. Peace. And deep, deep abiding love. *Abba* is a name that wraps its arms around you in a continuous embrace and never lets go. Are you there?

Do you believe you are God's beloved child just as much as Jesus is? A "child of God" who became his prized adopted son or daughter when you accepted Christ? How comfortable do you feel calling God *Abba*? Again, be totally honest with yourself. I cannot force it on you, and some of you may not be ready for it yet. That's okay—there's no condemnation if you aren't there.

I fooled myself for three decades that I was there when I really wasn't, so I understand. God's love for me personally just didn't seem real, like something I had to fake to fit in at church. It was almost too far out of my comfort zone because it was so "other-worldly." Three decades! It took me three decades to learn to rest in and receive his love. To understand that Jesus did it *all* for me. That I didn't have to prove myself. That he was the One who made me "worthy" of God's love, acceptance, and blessing. All my striving, all my good deeds, all the things I did for the kingdom—they were all fine. But relying on those things alone would never bring me peace. I would never be able to do enough to earn my salvation and God's total acceptance. I hope and pray you get there much sooner than I.

Leaning In

So, how do you come by this revelation of God's deep love for you? Well, how do you develop any relationship with someone you are serious about? Think about it in terms of the Song of Solomon, like a relationship between you and your fiancée. *You pursue her passionately!* You purposefully create time to be with her because she is your top priority. She's the one you want to be with. You talk to her about the things that mean the most to you in life and listen attentively to what she has to say. You share your dreams, what you hope your life with her will be like. You read and reread her love letters to you because they thrill your soul. And you prepare your heart for your forthcoming marriage.

Let's switch it back to God now. God's love letters to you are the books of the Bible. Every page drips with his love. Find a translation that is easy for you to understand, preferably a study Bible with explanatory notes at the bottom of the pages. Spend time in his presence. Listen for his voice. Get lost in worship, acknowledging his majesty and receiving his deep love for you. Declare his names until the glory and power of who he is connects with your inner being to become real. Prepare your heart by working through the issues I'm raising in this book so you can understand your identity in Christ better, so you can begin to see yourself with his eyes, and so you can love yourself with *his* love—that's loving yourself in a healthy way.

Seek out other Bible-based books which point you to inner healing. Hang out with believers who emanate the love of Christ and who can share of their own experiences in the Lord. Seek out wise Christian counselors and mentors. Ask God how you can grow best. Ask him how he *feels* about you! He will answer you, and I'm willing to bet you'll be surprised by his response.

I am talking about intentional, consistent, total immersion here of your mind, heart, and soul in the truths of God's goodness, his faithfulness, his strength working in you, and yes—in his love. Asking him to move the head knowledge of his love down into the depths of *your heart* is what transforms you. "Be transformed by the renewing of your mind" is how Romans 12:2 (NASB1995) puts it. Replacing the lies that came with your rejection or abandonment with the truths of who he is and who you are in Christ. (See appendix A for a list of identity declarations with Scripture references. *That* is the mirror you want to start looking in!)

This is what it comes down to, then. You don't have to live in fear of God any longer. Because of the cross, you will never be rejected. You will never be abandoned. Perfect love has come, and Perfect Love (Jesus!) shatters all fear. That includes the fear of rejection, of abandonment, and of punishment. He took it all to himself on the cross. It's all gone in our new covenant relationship with him.

And you don't have to live like a disconnected orphan any longer, either. Through the cross, you are no longer a slave to religious rules and regulations, needing to do things to prove how good you are to him. No more checklists of to-do's to earn God's favor. The specter of being on your own to survive life no longer has the power to haunt you. Through the risen Christ you have entered into the *shabbat* of God, the place of rest and peace, knowing he loves you just as much as his very own Son.

Servants watch from the sidelines as their master dines with his children. They eat the leftovers. Not you! God made a way for you to become a beloved child through Christ, with all the rights and privileges that go with that honor. You get to sit at his table and feast on his presence, to partake of his riches and grace towards you, and just to be … with him. To let him celebrate you. To receive his love. To enjoy his love. I feel it when Chandler Moore sings in "Jireh," "It doesn't take a trophy to make you proud … I'll never be more loved than I am right now." He's talking about *you*! You will never be more loved than you are right now.

I began this chapter with a quote from Romans 8:15–16. As we close, I'd like to go back to that passage but to *personalize* it specifically for you to say aloud. Consider taking a photo of it and posting it in a conspicuous place where you can read in and declare it every day. Do it. Let the words melt over your mind and heart as an anointing of a new day in your relationship with *Abba*. You'll never be more loved than you are right now:

> And I did not receive the "spirit of religious duty," leading me back into the fear of never being good enough. But I have received the "Spirit of full acceptance," enfolding me into the family of God. And I will never feel orphaned, for as he rises up within me, my spirit joins him in saying the words of tender affection, "Beloved [Abba]!" For the Holy Spirit makes God's fatherhood real to me as he whispers into my innermost being, "You are My beloved child!" (Romans 8:15–16, TPT)

My brother or sister in Christ, that is "deep calling to deep," the deep of the heart of God speaking to the deep of your soul. Grab hold of it! Believe it. Relish it. Receive God's love for what it is and overflow with gratitude at his amazing grace.

If you still have the dragons of rejection and the orphan spirit stalking you, the time has come for you to turn around and slay them. Be strong! Stand firm! Jesus defeated them for you two thousand years ago. The only power fear, anxiety, rejection, and abandonment have over you is the power you yield to them in your life. They don't belong to you anymore! Jesus cast them out when he went to the cross. You have been cleansed of it all by his power and grace, but only you can lay hold of what he has already provided.

Wait! What's that? Did you hear that? Listen! Do you recognize that voice? I *know* that voice. It's Jesus! His words echo loudly about us in this cavern. They reach into every crevice. They circle around every rock. They penetrate deep into the soul. Do you hear them? Listen! Listen …

"It is finished … It is finished!"

Selah.

Prayer

Father-God,

I come before you now, confessing that there have been times when I have been afraid of you because of what I have done or said or thought, because I thought you would punish me, reject me, or abandon me altogether. I reject those lies! I renounce that fear. I renounce rejection and abandonment. In Jesus's name, I cut myself free from the orphan spirit that has drawn me away from you, and I surrender myself to you once and for all.

Thank you that I do not have a spirit of fear, but of power and of love and of a sound mind. I bring my thoughts captive to you and the truths of Your Word. You promised us that you would not leave us as orphans, that you would send your Spirit to be with us, to guide us, to comfort us, to teach us, to encourage us, and to empower us to live the life you have for us. Thank you for the power of your Spirit doing a healing work deep within me.

Thank you, *Abba*, that I am your beloved child and nothing can ever change that. Open my heart and mind to the depth of your love for me. Help me to understand the cross and to stop striving to earn your love. To receive the fullness of the finished work of Jesus. To have a greater revelation that "it is finished" for me. So that I can be at peace. So that I can experience your pleasure and total acceptance. So that I can rest in your love.

In the mighty name of Jesus, I pray. Amen.

Key Summary Points:

- When the sin of Adam and Eve was "exposed" in the Fall, their true fear was that God would reject or abandon them so that they would never be able to enjoy his love again.

- True death is eternal separation from God, "but the free gift of God is eternal life in Christ Jesus our Lord" (Romans 6:23, NASB1995).

- "God has not given us a spirit of fear, but of power and of love and of a sound mind" (2 Timothy 1:7, NKJV).

- The orphan spirit is the fraternal twin to the fear of rejection or abandonment. It is characterized by relational difficulties, insecurity, a self-focus, and perfectionism.

- Lucifer was the original orphan by his own design. He is the great imitator. As God made us in his image, Lucifer tries to keep us conformed to *his* image—an orphan. But when we are born again, we are born as children into a new family, the family of God. No longer are we orphans.

- Jesus promised in John 14:18 that he would not leave us as orphans but would send the Holy Spirit to comfort, guide, and teach us all things. As a believer, the Spirit lives within you to empower you to overcome the fear of rejection and to be free from the orphan spirit.

- Jesus understands rejection so well. He was forsaken by family, close friends, and others when he went to the cross.

- God has promised us that he will never reject or abandon us (Hebrews 13:5–6).

- Only an abiding revelation of God's love from the deep of the heart of *Abba* to the deep of your own heart and soul will bring true freedom from the fear of rejection and the orphan spirit.

Reflection and Discussion Questions:

1. Thinking about Adam and Eve, describe a time when you felt naked, exposed in your sin before God. How did you react to the conviction of the Holy Spirit then? How would you respond now?

2. What is your greatest fear? What is the lie that underlies that fear? Express that fear to *Abba*. Renounce the lie and allow the rock-solid assurance of Jesus's love for you to replace the fear (1 John 4:18). (If in a group, consider answering these questions silently. Please be wise concerning how personal you get.)

3. Does knowing that Jesus, the Son of God himself, also experienced rejection, abandonment, betrayal, and being an orphan help you to believe that he understands what you're going through? How does that impact your trust level in God?

4. What does it mean to you that, in Christ, you are not an orphan, but an adopted son or daughter of a loving Father who is totally for you and fully invested in your well-being?

5. The New Testament tells us that we are in Christ when we put our faith in him. Keeping that in mind, do you truly believe that you are God's beloved child as much as Jesus is? Why or why not?

Afterward

His light broke through the darkness and he led us out in freedom from death's dark shadow and snapped every one of our chains. (Psalm 107:14, TPT)

When [Jesus] came to the front to read the Scriptures, he was handed the scroll of the prophet Isaiah. He unrolled the scroll and found where it is written, "The Spirit of the Lord is upon me, and he has anointed me to be hope for the poor, healing for the brokenhearted, and new eyes for the blind, and to preach to prisoners, 'You are set free!' I have come to share the message of [God's favor], for the time of God's great acceptance has begun." (Luke 4:17–19, TPT)

"Come away with Me …
It's not too late for you …
I have a plan for you
I have a plan for you
It's gonna be wild
It's gonna be great
It's gonna be full of Me
Open up your heart, and let Me in …"

(Brock Human from "Come Away" on the album *Come Away* by Jesus Culture © 2010 Capital Cmg Genesis, United Pursuit Music)

My family has been so blessed in recent years because we live a stone's throw away from hundreds of acres of beautiful conservation lands. We didn't even know they were there when we first moved in! The hills, forests, streams, and meadows have tons of trails meandering through them. Between hiking, cross-country skiing, and especially mountain biking, I've hit quite a few of those trails.

My exploration of this bucolic wonder has not been without incident, though. Early on, I would sometimes get lost, but just kept going until I found another trail that looked familiar. I have stumbled over thick tree roots hiding in the shadows multiple times. There was one day when I'm pretty sure I cracked a rib trying to cross-country ski on some very slick, ice-crusted snow. On a few occasions, the spirit of Superman came over me, and I went flying over the handlebars of my mountain bike into mud puddles, brush, or whatever. (Shhhh! Don't tell Jeanie!) I just laugh after these airborne mishaps because of how silly I look and how much fun I'm having. But in all my time of roaming those trails, I have yet to find a cave. Even if I did, I know I could easily figure my way out.

That's the way God intended life to be for us. Abundant. Joyful. Exciting. Fun. With him! Oh, we may stumble over things from time to time. We may take a bigger hit and crack a rib once in a while. Every now and then, we may even fly over the handlebars, crash, and come up looking pretty pathetic. But we're still on the trails! We're still moving forward! Jesus picks us up, washes the muck away, gives us a hug, and points us back to the path of living life because life is so different when we can trust him. When we trust him, we live life in abundance . . . in him, with him, and for him. When we are saturated with the love of Christ as we pass through the vagaries of life, we don't have to worry about hiding in any caves because the caves no longer hold power over us. The dark of the caves vanishes where the light of Jesus pulsates.

So, as our quest draws to a close, I have a question: How did this slice of your journey (reading this book) go for you? I hope well, overall. I pray you were able to take out some of your own dragons in the strength of the Spirit and exit those caves in victory. If you were only partially successful, good for you! You've made progress! You're moving forward, and that's really the most important thing. All of us who follow Jesus are on that same road with you. Even the apostle Paul declared that he hadn't "arrived."

If you want to go deeper into this material, you might consider rereading *Deep Calling to Deep* in a few weeks or a few months. That's how it is with inner healing—the Spirit helps you dig a little deeper each time. Remember Isaiah 42:3 (NASB1995), "A dimly burning wick He will not extinguish ..." As you diligently continue to seek God's face, he will change you. That dimly burning wick will transform into a roaring flame!

If, on the other hand, processing this material was just plain challenging, overwhelming, or maybe even too much for you, I can totally identify with that too. Going into the caves was traumatic for me personally. It took a long time. And it was tough because I had to face who I was with blunt truth if I wanted to grow in my relationship with God. Tough because I had to engage with where I had come from and look at a past I didn't want to look at. There was so much more buried there than I thought, and it was not pleasant. Tough because I had to wrestle with the lies I had been taught and believed about God and myself. Tough because of the work involved to reprogram my brain and heart with the truth of God's Word so that I could understand my identity in Christ better—as a dearly loved son of God. Jesus would never reject me or leave me. He would always be faithful to meet me where I was at.

It was especially tough because I felt betrayed by people I loved and trusted. People whom I thought could help lead me out of the caves because, even as a young boy, I felt so on my own. I knew I needed help. Oh, I get it; I get it. They didn't intentionally neglect me. They did the best they could. I don't hold anything against them. Really, I don't. I'm willing to bet you share some of those same sentiments.

But I would've been overjoyed if a few of the important people in my life had come alongside me to show more support and encouragement, to "show me the way" out of the caves in the way I needed. Parents. Authority figures in my life. Other leaders. The reality was that they *couldn't* help me much because, in their own woundedness, many of them were still wandering in the dark of their own caves. They still hadn't slain many of the dragons in their own lives.

But listen! Here's the good news, the "gospel" in all this! God sent us a Savior. You already know that Jesus experienced betrayal on every front right before he went to the cross. By the civil officials. By the religious authorities who refused to recognize him for who he was. By family. By his followers. By the closest of his friends, the disciples.

And Jesus paid the supreme price for all the good he had done. Death. Death in the most humiliating way—by crucifixion. When all the ridicule, shame, and crushing was over for Jesus, two of his disciples took his battered frame down from the cross. With great care, they tenderly wrapped his bruised, broken body in a shroud. Do you know what they did next? They laid him in

... a cave.

Oh! Oh, are you *seeing* this? It was a setup! A perfect setup by our great God! So similar to what had happened centuries earlier to the prophet Elijah on the side of Mt. Sinai. So, so similar. Except this time, it was different. The outcome was totally different because our Father-God, the deep love of who he is, spoke to the deep of the lifeless body of his Son, and this is what he whispered, "My Son. My dearly loved Son in whom I am so, so pleased. What are you doing ... *here*? Here is not *where* you're supposed to be. Here is not *who* you're supposed to be."

When our *Abba* uttered those words, the winds howled fiercely around the Calvary mount. The earth heaved in jolting waves. The fire of the Holy Spirit flashed in a torrent from the heavens, breathing new life into the motionless form of our Messiah. The stone rolled away, and Jesus walked out of

... the cave.

As a believer, you are in Christ. You are one with him now. That is new covenant relationship. You are a new creation![21] Now, listen—you have to get this because it is way beyond huge! You were in Christ even before the foundation of the world.[22] Your former self was crucified with him when you chose to follow him,[23] and you also walked out of the cave with him two thousand years ago.[24] Meditate for a bit on that. This is the deep of God speaking to the deep of your soul here.

Because you were *in* Christ, you walked out of that same dark cave *with* him two thousand years ago in his resurrection power. It's a done deal in the spirit realm! It is finished. You don't need to stay in the caves any longer. "It is finished" means you are done with the caves. It's over. The stone has been rolled away for you! The way out lies before you! Jesus did for you what you could not do for yourself. That is perfect love!

In his boundless gentleness and lovingkindness, however, our Jesus does not force you to follow him out of the dark enclaves within your heart. He grants you the freedom of how you will travel the trails he has set before you. But he will always continue to go after the sheep that is wandering, wherever that may be, including in the caves.

So, as this portion of your journey closes, I pray that, in *Deep Calling to Deep* …

> … you have had the courage to hear and heed the call of Father-God to venture into the caves of your heart.
>
> … that you have been able to slay your own dragons in the strength of Christ Jesus.
>
> … and that, under the guidance of the Holy Spirit, this book has enabled you to step out of the dark of the caves into the fullness of his marvelous resurrection light.

To see his goodness.
To receive his mercy.
To capture his grace.
To walk into freedom.

And to rest in his extravagant love. Forever.

I pray that you trust him enough now that, when you hear the deep of the heart of God whispering to the deep of your heart,

"I have a plan for you.

I have a plan for you.

It's gonna be wild.

It's gonna be great.

It's gonna be full of Me."

… you run to him with all that you are.

Congratulations!

You have just finished reading *Deep Calling to Deep: Overcoming the Struggles to Trust God* (book one).

I hope it has been a blessing to you. If you have found it to be helpful, let me encourage you to continue in this deeper journey of healing by reading and processing the material in books two and three of the Deeper Trilogy, when they become available.

An overview of their contents is as follows:

Book two of *Deep Calling to Deep* contains

> Chapter 3: Slaying the Demons Within: Offense at God
> Chapter 4: Offense and Victory in the Battles to Forgive

Book three contains

> Chapter 5: Slaying the Demons Without
> Chapter 6: Why We Can Trust God
> Chapter 7: Slaying the Last Demon Within: Doubt

Note: The introduction and afterward are the same for all three books of the Deeper Trilogy so that you can read each book as a separate work without necessarily reading the others, if so desired.

Other resources can be found at www.deepcallingtodeep.com.

Appendix A: Who I Am in Christ Jesus

(My Identity in Him)

- I am beloved of God. (1 Thessalonians 1:4)
- I am loved with an everlasting love. (Jeremiah 31:3)
- I am chosen of God. (1 Thessalonians 1:4)
- I am God's special creation, fearfully and wonderfully made in his image. (Psalm 139:14)
- I have been justified, "just as if I" had never sinned, completely forgiven in God's sight. (Romans 5:1)
- I died with Christ and died to the power of sin's rule over my life. (Romans 6:1–6)
- I am free forever from condemnation. (Romans 8:1)
- I have received the Spirit of God into my life that I might know the things freely given to me by God. (1 Corinthians 2:12)
- I have been reconciled to God. (2 Corinthians 5:18)
- I am a son or daughter of God. (Romans 8:14–15)
- I am the righteousness of God through Christ Jesus. (2 Corinthians 5:21)
- I have the mind of Christ. (1 Corinthians 2:16)
- I am sealed in Christ by the Holy Spirit. (Ephesians 1:13)
- I am a temple of the Holy Spirit. (1 Corinthians 6:19)
- I have direct access to God through the Spirit. (Ephesians 2:18)
- I am strong in the Lord. (Ephesians 6:10)
- I am victorious. (Revelations 21:7)
- I have overcome the world. (1 John 5:4)
- The One who lives in me is greater than the one who is in the world. (1 John 4:4)
- I am more than a conqueror through Christ Jesus. (Romans 8:37)
- I can do all things through Jesus Christ. (Philippians 4:13)

- I can love others with his love. (John 13:34–35)
- I am healed by the wounds of Jesus. (1 Peter 2:24)
- I have the peace of God which passes understanding. (Philippians 4:7)
- I have received the power of the Holy Spirit: power to lay hands on the sick and see them recover, power to cast out demons, and power over all the works of the enemy. (Mark 16:17)
- I shall do even greater works than Christ Jesus. (John 14:12)
- I have a spirit of power, love, and a sound mind. (2 Timothy 1:7)
- I am complete in Christ. (Colossians 2:10)
- I am overtaken by the blessings of God. (Deuteronomy 28:2)
- I have all my needs met by God according to his glorious riches in Christ Jesus. (Philippians 4:19)
- I am being changed into his image. (Philippians 1:6)
- I have a guaranteed inheritance. (Ephesians 1:14)
- I am united with Christ and one with him in spirit. (1 Corinthians 6:17)
- I cannot be separated from the love of God. (Romans 8:35)

Find your own Scripture promises. This is such a small list!

Appendix B: Making a Decision to Follow Christ

Making a conscious decision to follow Jesus Christ is the beginning of new spiritual life for you through the new relationship he established with us through his shed blood. This new relationship is found in the New Testament (or New Covenant) portion of the Bible. The Bible is clear in how it describes our human nature and what we need to do to be saved:

1. God desires the best for us in this life. "For I know the plans I have for you," says the Lord. "They are plans for good and not for disaster, to give you a future and a hope. In those days when you pray, I will listen. If you look for me wholeheartedly, you will find me" (Jeremiah 29:11–13, NLT).

2. But there is a problem—our sin separates us from God. "For all have sinned and fall short of the glory of God ..." (Romans 3:23, NASB1995). As we have seen, there is a price we must pay for our sin: "For the wages of sin is [spiritual] death ..." (Romans 6:23, NASB1995). Spiritual death refers to eternal separation from God when we die physically.

3. In his great grace and mercy, God provided Jesus as a substitute for us so that we would be spared the punishment of eternal death. "And since we have been made right in God's sight by the blood of Christ, he will certainly save us from God's condemnation. For since our friendship with God was restored by the death of his Son while we were still his enemies, we will certainly be saved through

the life of his Son. So now we can rejoice in our wonderful new relationship with God because our Lord Jesus Christ has made us friends of God" (Romans 5:9–11, NLT).

4. We cannot earn salvation through our own good works during our time on this earth. It is not a matter of our good deeds tipping a balance in our favor with God. Salvation is a free gift from God that we receive by faith. "For it was only through this wonderful grace that we believed in him. Nothing we did could ever earn this salvation, for it was the gracious gift from God that brought us to Christ! So no one will ever be able to boast, for salvation is never a reward for good works or human striving" (Ephesians 2:8–9, TPT).

5. It is important that you verbally confess what you believe and tell someone about it. "In fact, it says, 'The message is very close at hand; it is on your lips and in your heart.' And that message is the very message about faith that we preach: If you openly declare that Jesus is Lord and believe in your heart that God raised him from the dead, you will be saved. For it is by believing in your heart that you are made right with God, and it is by openly declaring your faith that you are saved" (Romans 10:8–10, NLT).

If you believe what I shared above, use your own words to pray to God along these lines:

Father-God,

You are a good and merciful God. I realize and acknowledge now that I am a sinner and need you in my life. By faith, I accept your Son Jesus as my Lord and the One who saves me from the penalty of my sin through his death and resurrection.

Thank you for washing me clean of all the times I have failed you. I ask you now to baptize me in your Holy Spirit to empower me to live the abundant life you desire for me.

I pray this in the mighty name of Jesus. Amen.

Bibliography

Bible Gateway. Accessed December 5, 2022. https://www.biblegateway.com.

Blue Letter Bible. Accessed December 7, 2022. https://www.blueletterbible.org.

Brown, Brené. "The Power of Vulnerability." June 2010. Houston. TEDxHouston. http://www.ted.com/talks/brene_brown_on_vulnerability.html.

"The Consequences of Fatherlessness," Encouragement, Support, and Guidance. Accessed November 11, 2019. http://www.fathers.com/statistics-and-research/the-consequences-of-fatherlessness.

Dwomoh, Ivy, and Elaine Dinolfo. "Effects of Homelessness on Children," *Pediatrics in Review* 39 (2018): 530. http://www.pedsinreview.aappublications.org/content/39/10/530.

Engel, Beverly. "Healing Your Shame and Guilt Through Self-Forgiveness," *Psychology Today*, June 1, 2017. Available at www.psychologytoday.com/us/blog/the-compassion-chronicles/201706/healing-your-shame-and-guilt-through-self-forgiveness.

Goewey, Don Joseph. "85 Percent of What We Worry About Never Happens." *HuffPost*. August 25, 2015. Accessed November 13, 2019. https://www.huffpost.com/entry/85-of-what-we-worry-about_b_8028368?guccounter.

Heitland, Leif. *Healing the Orphan Spirit* (Rev. Ed.). Peachtree City, GA: Global Mission Awareness, 2013.

Human, Brock. "Come Away." April 2009. Track 4 on *Radiance*. © 2011 United Pursuit Records.

Kämmerer, Annette. "The Scientific Underpinnings and Impacts of Shame." *Scientific American*. August 9, 2019. Accessed April 25, 2020. www.scientificamerican.com/article/the-scientific-underpinnings-and-impacts-of-shame/.

"The Making of a Fatherless Daughter" (video). The Fatherless Daughters Network—"Inspiring One Million Women to Flourish Beyond Fatherlessness." Accessed November 17, 2019. http://www.fatherlessdaughters.net/.

Mattera, Joseph. "13 Traits of 'Orphan Spirit' Leaders." Charisma News, *The Pulse*. September 29, 2016. Accessed November 19, 2019. http://www.charismanews.com/opinion/the-pulse/60227-13-traits-of-orphan-spirit-leaders.

"The Proof Is In: Father Absence Harms Children." National Fatherhood Initiative. No date. Available at https://www.fatherhood.org/father-absence-statistic. Accessed November 17, 2019.

Robinson, Rich. "Jesus' References to Old Testament Scriptures." May 16, 2017. Accessed November 15, 2019. https://www.jewsforjesus.org/answers/jesus-references-to-old-testament-scriptures/ .

Schwartz, Allan N., Ph.D. "Psychological Issues Faced by Adopted Children and Adults." Accessed November 18, 2019. https://www.mentalhelp.net/parenting'psychological-issues-faced-by-adopted-children-and-adults/.

Sowers, John. *Fatherless Generation*. Grand Rapids, MI: Zondervan, 2010.

"Spiritual Warfare: Defeating Guilt and Shame," Accessed November 8, 2017. http://www.greatbiblestudy.com/sws_guilt_shame.php.

Wickham, Phil. "Heart Full of Praise." Recorded June 2021. Track 13 on *Hymn of Heaven*. © 2021 Essential Music Publishing.

Acknowledgments

Pastors Zenzo and Michelle Matoga, and Pastors Femi and Sayo Adeduji—thank you for your courageous leadership and for the desire to bring freedom to the body of Christ, especially at Impact Church.

And to all those in Epic Journey, the best small group in the world! Your heart for God fuels my passion to share the transforming truths of this book.

Wayne and Kathy Wirtanen, Cisco Ducasse, Igor and Leila Almeida, Mariana Garces, and Jen Aldana—thank you for your willingness to speak the truth in love about what would improve *Deep Calling to Deep*, however tough it may have been for me to hear at times!

Chris and Lexi Cherry, Joe and Tammy Lynch, Prof. Ababa Abiem, and Keree-Ann Waite—thank you for your prayer, support, and encouragement.

Josh and Carolyn Vizzaco—thank you for your kindness and for a magnificent cover.

The many at WestBow Press who put this all together—thank you! You are amazing!

Notes

Chapter 1

What the Enemy Is After

1   See Hebrews 4:12.

2   See John 8:44.

3   See John 10:10.

4   See Mark 4:13-20.

5   See Romans 12:2.

6   See John 6:63; Luke 10:1-21; Matthew 24:35.

7   See 1 John 3:8 and John 10:10.

True Guilt

8   A pack of gum or Necco wafers cost 5 cents back then! After being off the market for years, Necco wafers became available online and at select stores again in 2020, in case you were wondering!

9   This example illustrates what happened to one of our sons a few years back. He was conflicted about declaring his tips, but did so. Several years later he was blessed with a high-paying job.

The Deep of Shame—Going to Its Core

10   Brené Brown, "The Power of Vulnerability," June 2010, Houston.TEDxHouston, http://www.ted.com/talks/brene_brown_on_vulnerability.html.

11   Brown, "The Power of Vulnerability."

Chapter 2

Roots of Fear

12   Unfortunately, I have occasionally seen this type of situation occur.

Fear of Rejection or Abandonment

13   This list represents combined data from: "The Proof Is In: Father Absence Harms Children," accessed November 17, 2019, https://www.fatherhood.

org/father-absence-statistic and "The Consequences of Fatherlessness," accessed November 17, 2019, http://www.fathers.com/statistics-and-research/the-consequences-of-fatherlessness.

14 "The Making of a Fatherless Daughter" (video), accessed November 17, 2019, http://www/fatherlessdaughters.net/.

The Orphan Spirit

15 Though the material in this section is original in great part, there are several thoughts which I expand upon which were originally derived from Leif Hetland's book, Healing the Orphan Spirit [Revised Edition].

16 Lucifer used the same, twisted deception on Adam and Eve that he fell prey to: "You shall be like God [when you eat of the fruit]."

17 Scholars believe that Isaiah 14:12–15 is a hidden glimpse of Lucifer's thoughts and actions before he was banished from the heavenlies. Also, see Luke 10:18.

Recognizing the Orphan Spirit

18 I cannot "prove" this claim because "orphan spirit" is not a medical term. Therefore, no particular research study exists relating orphan spirit to other psychosocial problems.

Jesus Feels Our Pain

19 I understand the context of this verse pertains to Jesus being tempted by sin in the same way we are tempted, but I also believe he can sympathize and identify with us in so many other dimensions of our humanity.

20 Luke 1:26–56, NASB1995.

Afterward

21 See Romans 6–7 and Galatians 2:19–20.

22 See Matthew 25:34 and Ephesians 1:4, for example.

23 See Galatians 2:20.

24 See Ephesians 2:6 and Colossians 2:12.

Printed in the United States
by Baker & Taylor Publisher Services